RACIAL ISSUES

revised printing

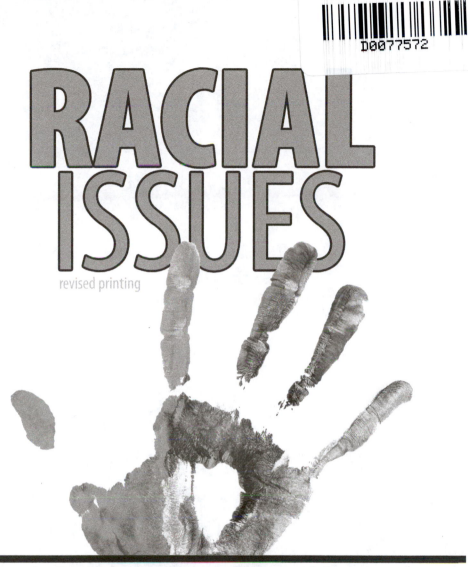

St. Cloud State University Racial Issues Colloquium

with contributions by:
Jeanne A. Lacourt, Ph.D., LPC(MS), NCC, Coordinator, RIC at SCSU
Mark Jaede, Ph.D., Luke Tripp, Ph.D., Margaret Villanueva, Ph.D.

Kendall Hunt
publishing company

Contents

PART I

What Are Race, Ethnicity, and Racialization?

Margaret Villanueva, Ph.D.

What is "Race"?

To ask what "race" means is to explore the history of racism. The notion that human beings are separated into categories of "race" is a recent idea in world history, yet one that profoundly affects everyone in the United States today. Even if we understand and acknowledge that all people are *homo sapiens* and thus biologically the same species, we are left with a deep seated notion about "difference" that is grounded in the social, cultural, and institutional relationships of "race" that gradually developed over 300 years in the United States and Europe.

Like other people growing up in Western cultures, we take for granted that everyone in the world belongs to a "race," and these customary patterns of thought are not easily overcome through reason or scientific knowledge. Modern science tells us that "race as a biological concept cannot be supported by the facts that we have learned about human biophysical variations and their genetic

1

basis" (Smedley & Smedley 2012, 3). "Race" is not real—yet, becoming aware that "race" was merely a human invention is only the first step in overcoming systemic racism.

To unravel what "race" means, we must take note of how "race" and "racism" mutually support each other. However, living in a society constructed around racial categories makes it difficult to step "outside" ourselves to evaluate our relationships and institutions objectively. Like characters in *The Matrix,* we are so accustomed to living "inside" a world constructed around invisible notions and operations of "race," that we cannot imagine what that world might look like from the outside. Simply claiming "I don't see race" will not reveal the inner workings of the racialized social construction that surrounds us; like the hero of *The Matrix,* to take a step outside and face a stark reality requires courage and struggle.

"What came first, 'race' or 'racism'?" is a circular puzzle impossible to answer. Systemic racism is "a system of social advantages and disadvantages based on race" (Tatum 2003), and the power to categorize people as belonging to distinct "races" based on physical characteristics was exercised by white European Americans. As European economic and political power expanded across the Americas, a "science of race" was invented to justify a system of racial domination and subordination in a country that declared "liberty and justice for all."

In the British colonies of the 1600s, Irish and African servants and agricultural laborers worked side-by-side, intermarried, and were not treated differently based on "race" but based on their subservient class status (Smedley & Smedley 2012, 102–5). But by 1776, when Thomas Jefferson wrote that "all men are created equal" in the Declaration of Independence, he and other authors of the Constitution were slaveholders. How could they explain the contradiction between their ideals of human freedom and a system of human slavery? The idea of "race" justified the violent dispossession of native peoples from their lands, and the expanding enslavement of African people in the prosperous plantation economy. Notions of white supremacy on one hand, and racial inferiority on the other, sustained the social and cultural advantages of being "white" in the United States from the 1700s through the Civil Rights era of the mid-twentieth century.

Anthropologist Audrey Smedley points out that by the late-eighteenth century, when Americans declared their independence from Britain, Europeans assumed that all human groups were ranked in a great "Chain of Being." These preconceived notions informed the scientific research of the day, at a time when scientists "turned to the physical characteristics of the Indian as well as the black population" (Smedley & Smedley 2012, 165). The "natural order" that scientists found was a mirror image of the emerging socioeconomic order where people of European descent ruled over other peoples. Smedley argues that by turning to the science of race differences, "white Americans looked for explications and justifications for their practices and policies in what they thought were the intrinsic characteristics of the Indians themselves" (Smedley & Smedley 2012, 166).

Classification of people by "race" leads to a question about the status of mixed-race people, which in modern scientific understanding means all peoples of the world, there being no scientific evidence for any biological "separation of the races" in the genetic past of *homo sapiens.* We know that the child of a parent from Africa and a parent from Europe would share equally in the genetic ancestry of both parents. However, in the United States since the time of Jefferson, "race" has been defined socially, never simply as a matter of biology or genetic heritage. For example, the assumption about racial identities (confused with what today we would consider "ethnic" identities) in 1916 would be that

> The cross between a white and an Indian is an Indian; the cross between a white man and a negro is a negro; the cross between a white and a Hindu is a Hindu; and the cross between any of the three European races and a Jew is a Jew. (Madison Grant cited in Marks 1995, 111)

In the race-based society of the early United States, slaveholders like Jefferson could father "mixed-race" children, yet could distance themselves from acknowledging kinship with their enslaved offspring. Smedley (2012, 183–4) points out that the social construction of race in 1800 was so stringent and the dichotomy of free/white and unfree/black was so well established, that Jefferson "could not even recognize his own children, emotionally, psychologically, or socially" because the social construction of race meant that "he could retain the conviction that slaves, even his own children, were qualitatively different and inferior kinds of being."

How is "Race" Connected to "Racism"?

Despite the deep-seated divisions of US society along racial lines, and a history of "race" categories being enforced through science, law, and other social arrangements, today we hear charges of "racism" directed at public figures such as the first African American president or the first Latina Supreme Court justice. How do we make sense of the way that terms like "racism" or "racist" make their way into media and popular culture as we enter the twenty-first century?

Sociologists Michael Omi and Howard Winant (1994, 69–70) point out that after the Civil Rights movements of the 1960s, the meaning of "racism" has been eroding and losing its critical force as a concept, or it has been challenged by the notion of "color-blindness." On one hand, in 1960, it would have been impossible to imagine electing a Black president, or appointing a Puerto Rican woman to the Supreme Court. On the other hand, it would have been unimaginable to hear a white person accuse a Black, Latino, American Indian or Asian person of "racism" in public or on the media, given the prevailing forms of discrimination that placed people of color at an obvious disadvantage compared to the white population. In a period when black protesters in the South were attacked by police dogs or knocked over by fire hoses, television viewers across the country watched scenes of violence intended to stifle dissent and frighten the youth back into submission. But the attackers were unaware that their displays of violence would turn the tide against Jim Crow laws and a system of official racism.

According to Beverly Tatum (1997), and many social science researchers, "systemic racism" in the United States is a system of advantages for white European Americans, and a system of disadvantages for Americans of color. Before the 1960s, racism had been understood as individual prejudices that could lead to discrimination against "minorities." Beginning with the organized protests by Black, Chicano, Puerto Rican, American Indian, and Asian activists during the 1960s to the early 1970s, the United States took notice of our history of racial injustices, with civil rights laws being passed under Presidents Kennedy and Johnson. As a result of these social movements, we now understand that

> Discrimination, far from manifesting itself only (or even principally) through individual actions or conscious policies, was a structural feature of U.S. society, the product of centuries of systematic exclusion, exploitation, and disregard of racially defined minorities. (Omi & Winant 1994, 69)

Several decades later, a period of political backlash has limited efforts to address racial inequalities and institutional discrimination. Although race relations have become more complex and we have experienced progress in many areas, we still face housing segregation, racial disparities in health and educational outcomes, growing inequalities in family wealth between black and white households or white and Latino households, racial profiling by police, unequal rates of incarceration, and an increase in hate groups and hate crimes since 2000.

In formulating the concept of "racial formation," Omi and Winant (1994, 73–5) point out that the concept of "race" is not fixed, nor is "racism" either solely psychological or cultural (ideological), or located only in unjust practices and institutions (structural). Rather, the racial "ideology and social structure . . . mutually shape the nature of racism in a complex, dialectical, and overdetermined manner."

Considered in this light, we are better able to compare the term "ethnicity" to the concept of "race." Both are social constructions or ways of categorizing human individuals and groups. It is important to understand the historical differences in the two terms, but also how they may overlap when thinking about our everyday lives and social worlds.

What is "Ethnicity"?

"Race" was a "new form of social differentiation" in human history, emerging between the seventeenth and eighteenth centuries in Europe and the American colonies. We trace the notion of "ethnic" peoples back to Ancient Greece, contrasting "others" (*ethnos*) or the non-Greek peoples of the Mediterranean world in contrast to those who belonged to Greek society (*polis*). Academic studies of "ethnic groups" were reactions to the arrival of poor European immigrants in 1920s and 1930s. Although "race" and "ethnicity" are both socially constructed ways of understanding human differences, "race" refers to physical characteristics or supposedly inherent biological traits, while "ethnicity" refers primarily to cultural differences:

> Ethnicity itself was understood as the result of a group formation process based on culture and descent. 'Culture' in this formulation included such diverse factors as religion, language, 'customs,' nationality, and political identification. 'Descent' involved heredity and a sense of group origins. . . . (Omi & Winant 1994, 15)

Unlike the social construction of "race" that focused on Jefferson's questions of inherent superiority or inferiority of human "races," the early twentieth century sociologists wanted to understand whether the new immigrants would "assimilate" and "melt" into the dominant white Anglo Saxon protestant population, or whether the "cultural pluralism" of ethnic immigrants would have an impact on American society. Given these questions, the difficulties and lower social status faced by people defined by their "race"—the Africans, Mexicans, Asians, or Native Americans—were often blamed on those people themselves. People of color were compared negatively to the European ethnic groups who eventually achieved social mobility (often through ethnic solidarity and mutual support rather than through conformity or individual efforts):

> If Chicanos don't do well in school, this cannot, even hypothetically, be due to low-quality education; it has instead to do with Chicano values. After all, Jews and Japanese Americans did well in inferior schools, so why can't other groups? (Omi & Winant 1994, 21)

Smedley and Smedley explain that although "ethnicity" and a sense of "ethnocentrism" or strong preferences for ones' own language, beliefs, customs, and values may divide people across many regions of the world, the idea of "race" is a much more powerful source of division. By the 1950s, most of the distinct European "ethnic groups" in the United States had become part of mainstream American society—while people perceived as racially distinct continue to be treated differently no matter how many generations they have lived in the country. Where European Americans are a historical majority, such as in the rural Midwest, the sense of an "ethnic" identity based on country of origin have often been forgotten. After several generations, "white" people lose sight of their ethnic origins, yet they seldom think of themselves specifically as a "racial" group, but as the "norm" (Tatum 1997), as simply "Americans." On the other hand, the ethnic diversity of African Americans has never been noticed within the United States, because the idea of "race" meant that they were all considered to be and treated alike as a "Negro" or black race (Omi & Winant 1994, 22).

As the dominant population, white Europeans, particularly Anglo Saxons, not only invented the idea of "race" but held power over the land and labor of the peoples who they forced into these categories. "Ethnic groups" from Europe might gradually assimilate to the dominant society, but peoples defined by "race" above and beyond their "ethnicity," faced legal, economic, and political forms of discrimination—forced labor, exclusion, dispossession, and genocide. The resulting low social status of peoples of color was then "explained" by the notion of racial superiority and inferiority.

Although European colonists "ignored the cultural and physical diversity among Native Americans and homogenized them all into a single group of more or less "savage Indians" (Smedley & Smedley 2012, 315), today American Indian survivors are taking back their history and renewing their cultures, describing themselves in terms of place and heritage. Yet extreme poverty, ecological destruction, and resentment continue to plague American Indian communities. Mixed or "mestizo" Latin Americans have been categorized racially through their Indian or African descent, and under some circumstances as "white," but the category of "Hispanic/Latino" is reflected on the Census as a separate "ethnic" category—with a request for individuals to self-identify by "race" in a second Census question. Despite the official uncertainty about Latino racial/ethnic status, across their 400 years of encounters with Anglo Americans, a long process of "racialization" justified the conquest of Mexican and Puerto Rican territories between 1848 and 1898, the confiscation of Mexican American and Puerto Rican lands, and reinforced images of both racial and cultural inferiority that designated a "commodity identity" for Mexican laborers and immigrants in low-paid sectors of the US economy (Vélez-Ibáñez 1996). For Puerto Ricans, their status of US citizens since 1898 and 1917 is barely recognized when they migrate to the mainland, and their social position in urban areas resembles that of African Americans with the added insult of being treated as "foreigners."

Similarly, even though the Census Bureau has asked people of Asian descent about their ethnic or national identities (Filipino, Korean, Vietnamese), the category of "Asian American" is clearly racial. Although European ethnic immigrants faced discrimination, the notion of the "lower races of Europe" was overcome with the fight against Fascism during World War II and the growth of post-war multi-ethnic white suburbs. However, for Asian Americans, the early 1940s were marked by increasing racial animosity, such as the internment of Japanese first- and second-generation residents. Audrey Smedley points out that

> Wherever there were visible physical and/or cultural differences among new immigrants to the United States, the potential for the stigma of racial inferiority could be, and usually was, applied. For white Americans, power and status relationships had to be established . . . (thus) the antagonism toward the Chinese began as early as 1852, and by 1870 organized protests against the 'mongolian hordes' were taking place. . . . The racialization of the Chinese had begun. (Smedley & Smedley 2012, 245)

Omi & Winant state that even though they "should be able to maintain their ethnic identities and thus avoid 'racialization'. . . . The majority of Americans cannot tell the difference between members of various (Asian) groups. . . ."

> (Asian Americans) are racially identified—their identities are racially constructed—by processes far more profound than mere state policy formation. (Omi & Winant 1994, 23)

As the twentieth century drew toward a close, challenges to the accomplishments of the Civil Rights Era were gaining steam. Biologist Stephan Jay Gould wrote about a resurgence of popular and quasi scientific notions of "race" at the time:

> . . . I was inspired to write this book because biological determinism is rising in popularity again, as it always does in times of political retrenchment. . . . Millions of people are now suspecting that their social prejudices are scientific facts after all. Yet these latent prejudices themselves, not fresh data, are the primary source of renewed attention. . . . Few tragedies can be more extensive than the stunting of life, few injustices deeper than the denial of an opportunity to strive or even to hope, by a limit imposed from without, but falsely identified as lying within. (Gould 1981, 28)

Are we finding that Dr. Gould's words ring true decades later, when we observe a President who ran on a campaign of "hope" finding himself disrespected during official appearances, and his personal identity and integrity questioned in coded racial terms? In the first decades of the twenty-first century, we are faced with challenges to the 1965 Voters' Rights Act across the country, a surge in hate crimes and xenophobia such as the massacre at a Sikh temple near Milwaukee, and daily news about communities protesting the killings of unarmed Black or Latino men by police officers or vigilantes. Even though the younger generation did not create a world where social advantages and disadvantages are distributed along racial and ethnic lines, this is the world we still inhabit, and today's college generation again has an opportunity to learn about, acknowledge, and turn against racism.

References

Gould, Stephen Jay, 1981. *The Mismeasure of Man,* New York: W.W. Norton & Company.

Marks, Jonathan, 1995. *Human Biodiversity: Genes, Race, and History,* New York: Aldine de Gruyter.

Omi, Michael & Howard Winant, 1994. *Racial Formation in the United States: From the 1960s to the 1990s,* New York: Routledge.

California Newsreel, 2003. *Race: The Power of an Illusion.* PBS: http://www.pbs.org/race/000 General/000 00-Home.htm

Smedley, Audrey & Brian D. Smedley, 2012. *Race in North America: Origin and Evolution of a Worldview,* Boulder, CO: Westview Press.

Tatum, Beverly D., 1997. *"Why Are All the Black Kids Sitting Together in the Cafeteria?" and Other Conversations on Race,* Basic Books.

Vélez-Ibáñez, Carlos, 1996. *Border Visions: Mexican Cultures of the Southwest,* Tucson: University of Arizona Press.

CHAPTER 1

Race as a Worldview:
A Theoretical Perspective

Audrey Smedley, Ph.D. and Brian Smedley, Ph.D.

Race as a Worldview: A Theoretical Perspective

The primary thesis of this book—and what the research has shown—is that *race* was from its inception a folk classification, a product of popular beliefs about human differences that evolved from the sixteenth through the nineteenth centuries. As a worldview, it was a cosmological ordering system structured out of the political, economic, and social experiences of peoples who had emerged as expansionist, conquering dominating nations on a worldwide quest for wealth and power. By a folk classification, I refer to the ideologies, distinctions, and selective perceptions that constitute a society's popular imagery and interpretations of the world. People in all societies comprehend the world through prisms that their cultures and experiences proffer to them. They impose meanings on new discoveries and experiences that emanate from their own cultural conditioning and interpret these realities in terms with which they are familiar. One of the first examples of this described in this book is the way the English fabricated an image of savagery from their experiences with the Irish and then imposed this image on Native Americans and later Africans.

Like all elements of culture, the racial worldview is dynamic, subject to oscillations in its expression and interpretation, from time to time intensified or contracted, sometimes modified and/or reinvented in response to changing circumstances. It also manifests contradictions and inconsistencies as life experiences, various social forces, and new knowledge provoke subtle modifications in attitudes about human differences. In the United States, the racial worldview has waxed and waned largely in response to economic forces that alter the conditions of labor competition and political realities that from time to time have incorporated or advanced the interests of the low-status races.

Race, then, originated not as a product of scientific investigation but as a folk concept; it initially had no basis, no point of origin, in science or naturalistic studies. The folk idea was subsequently embraced, beginning in the mid- to late-eighteenth century, by naturalists and other learned people and given credence and legitimacy as a supposed product of scientific investigation. The scientists themselves undertook efforts to document the existence of the differences that the European cultural worldview demanded and had already created. In their efforts to promote a valid basis for the idea of race, scientists not only reflected the biases, beliefs, and conditioning of their times, but, as in the cases of Louis Agassiz in the nineteenth century and Sir Cyril Burt in the twentieth, they often expressed their own personal fears, prejudices, and aesthetic evaluations of peoples whom they saw as alien. That their judgments and scientific conclusions mirrored popular beliefs should come as no surprise. As John Greene (1981) has shown, science is inevitably shaped by existing knowledge, values, beliefs, and presuppositions.

From its first continuous application to human populations during the eighteenth century, *race* was a way of categorizing what were already conceived of as inherently unequal human populations. Indeed, had all human beings been considered at least potentially equal by European explorers and exploiters, there would have been no need for the concept of race at all. People could have continued to be identified in the ways that had been employed ever since the first distinct groups came into contact with one another—that is, by their own names for themselves (their ethnic names); by the categorizing terms such as *people, group, society,* and *nation;* or by labels taken from the geographic region or locales they inhabited. Separateness and inequality are central to the idea of race.

By the early decades of the nineteenth century, the race concept in North America contained at least five ascertainable ideological ingredients, which, when taken together, may be considered diagnostic of race in the United States. Some were reflections of presuppositions deeply embedded in English culture and history; others were relatively new ideas that appeared with the colonial and slavery experiences but were compatible with the values, beliefs, and interests of the leaders of, especially, the southern colonies. When combined, these formed a singular paradigm constituting the racial worldview.

The first and most basic element was a universal classification of human groups as exclusive and discrete biological entities. The classifications were not based on objective variations in language or culture, but rather eclipsed these attributes and included superficial assessments and value judgments of phenotypic and behavioral variations. The categories were arbitrary and subjective and often concocted from the impressions, sometimes fanciful, of remote observers. A second element, emphasized above, was the imposition of an inegalitarian ethos that required the ranking of these groups vis-à-vis one another. Ranking was an intrinsic, and explicit, aspect of the classifying process, derived from the ancient model of the Great Chain of Being (a hierarchical structure of all living things; see chapter 7), which had been adapted to eighteenth-century realities.

A third element of North American race ideology was the belief that the outer physical characteristics of human populations were but surface manifestations of inner realities, for example, the cognitive linking of physical features with behavioral, intellectual, temperamental, moral, and other qualities. Thus, what today most scholars recognize as cultural (learned) behavior was seen as an innate concomitant of biophysical form. A fourth element was the notion that all of these qualities were inheritable—the biophysical characteristics, the cultural or behavioral features and capabilities, and the social rank allocated to each group by the belief system itself. Finally, perhaps the most critical element of all was the belief that each exclusive group (race) was created unique and distinct by nature or God, so that the imputed differences, believed to be fixed and unalterable, could never be bridged or transcended.

The synthesis of these elements constituted the folk concept and worldview of race in America, when this term began to replace other classificatory terms and to be widely used in the English language during the eighteenth century. The ideology enveloped in the concept was universal, comprehensive, and infinitely expandable. By the nineteenth century, all human groups of varying degrees of biological and/or cultural diversity could be subsumed arbitrarily into some racial category, depending on the objectives or goals of those establishing the classifications.

Once structured on a hierarchy of inequality, different races became socially meaningful wherever the term was used and to whatever groups it could be extended. Attitudes, beliefs, myths, and assumptions about the world's peoples, developed during the period of greatest European expansion and exploitation of non-European lands and peoples, were embroidered into systematic ideologies about their differing capacities for civilization and progress. All colonial peoples were seen as distinct races, all had to be ranked somewhere below whites, and even some Europeans had to be divided into racial groups and ranked.

As it evolved in the nineteenth century, the concept of race posed a new dimension of social differentiation that superseded "class." Race offered a new mechanism for structuring society based on a conception of naturally fixed, heritable, and immutable status categories linked to visible physical markers. The idea of "natural" inequality was a central component of race from its inception, but few recognized this as a mere analog of social position transformed into myth. Devout Christians saw it as God-ordained, and the irreligious rationalized the inequality as a fundamental part of "natural laws." In the same century, racial groups began to be confirmed in their inequalities by science, which cast their imagery to reflect the unquestioned verities of the dominant society's beliefs. Finally, the legal apparatus of the United States and various state governments conspired with science to legitimize this structural inequality by sanctioning it in law. Thus, the racial worldview was institutionalized and made a systemic and dominant component of American social structure.

This cultural construction of race as social reality reached full development in the latter half of the nineteenth century. After the Civil War, it was utilized as a social device to transform the freed black population of the North American continent into a subordinate, subhuman caste. It was further used to degrade and brutalize the Native American peoples and establish specific social parameters for other, newer immigrants, including the Irish, who had first experienced some of the elementary features of the racial worldview (see chapter 3).

In the nineteenth and early twentieth centuries, the idea of race differences was seized upon to divide, separate, and rank European populations and justify the dominance of certain class groups or ethnic elements. This led inexorably to the mass terror, incalculable atrocities, and genocide of Nazi race ideology and practices. These events had a major impact on American social consciousness and generated growing antiracist sentiments among a populace prepared by its own ideals to combat Nazism. Also in the twentieth century, the state of South Africa came much closer to realizing and operationalizing the mandates of this worldview under its system of apartheid.

The legacy of the historical development of the idea of race has been the retention into the twenty-first century of the folk sense of fundamental differences and inequality between peoples classified as separate races. It persists as an unarticulated reality despite recent developments in the biological sciences, which, as we shall see, have failed to confirm the existence of differences between groups greater in magnitude than those found between individuals. The idea of race continues in large part because of its value as a mechanism for identifying who should have access to wealth, privilege, loyalty, respect, and power, and who should not. And of course, for some individuals in the high-status race, it is a powerful psychological force, providing scapegoat functions as well as a facile external means of establishing and measuring one's self-worth. Race became, and still is, the fulcrum and symbol of a worldview and ideology that promotes an easy and simple explanation for human history and progress, or the lack thereof. Most important, it declares a kind of ordered structure to society that appears to be grounded in the very diversity created by nature.

This is the story that this book tells, but it is not an easy one to learn.

Race and Ethnicity: Biology and Culture

As we have seen, a fundamental dichotomy made by modern anthropologists and other scholars is that between culture and biology. We emphasize that culture is a learned behavior that varies independently of the physical characteristics of the people who carry it. People who live and interact together in a common community develop lifestyles, value orientations, language styles, customs, beliefs, and habits that differ from those of their neighbors. Over large geographic areas, variations in language and cultural traits may become quite noticeable, so that populations may differ radically from one another even within the same political community. People who share cultural characteristics, such as religion, a common cultural history, a group name and identity, and language traits, see themselves as distinct from other populations. A modern way of expressing the common interests of people who are perceived by others and themselves as having the same culture is to speak of them as an *ethnic group*. When ethnic groups evolve values that project their own lifestyles as superior to the cultures of others, we identify such attitudes as *ethnocentric* (or chauvinistic).

It is important at the outset to have a clear understanding of the difference between race and racism on the one hand, and ethnicity and ethnocentrism on the other. These terms reflect conceptually, and realistically, quite different kinds of phenomena and their use should be so restricted in the interest of accurate communication. It is unfortunate that the languages of the sciences, particularly the social sciences, have sometimes tended to proliferate and obfuscate meanings rather than provide precision and clarity. *Ethnicity* is one of those relatively modern terms that has sometimes been hailed as a suitable substitute for *race,* but that has also itself taken on a confusing plethora of meanings and nuances. Just one of the meanings listed in *Webster's New International Dictionary* shows how imprecise and impracticable the term can be; *ethnicity* is defined as "racial, linguistic, and cultural ties with a specific group." Ethnicity is a quality of ethnic groups, and *ethnic* itself seems to be almost anything and everything. The automatic linkage of biology and behavior (culture) in our collective consciousness obviously precipitated the inclusion of "racial ties" (here seen as physical traits) and the confusion of these very different domains.

Somewhat more sanguine about how we deal with physical, psychological, linguistic, and cultural phenomena, anthropologists have been cautious to relate the terms *ethnic* and *ethnicity* to real, as well as perceived, cultural differences between peoples. Nowadays, "culture" is defined, following E. B. Tylor's inclusive and unsurpassed rendering, as "that complex whole which includes knowledge, belief, art, morals, law, custom, and any other capabilities and habits acquired by man as a member of society" ([1871] 1958, 1). In our time, we would substitute *human beings* for *man* and emphasize the term *acquired.* The point is very simple: Culture is learned, not inborn, behavior; it refers to ways of behaving and thinking that we learn as we grow up in any society. It also refers to the things we learn when we adapt to or assimilate features of a different culture. *Ethnic* and *ethnicity* are best used to refer to all those traditions, customs, activities, beliefs, and practices that pertain to a particular group of people who see themselves and are seen by others as having distinct cultural features, a separate history, and a specific sociocultural identity. It is important to note that members of an ethnic group need not have common physical traits.

On occasion we have all used certain physical attributes of individuals as clues to their nationality or geographic origins, such as, for example, in the identification of East Indians or Asians. But physical characteristics do not automatically proclaim the *cultural* background or behavior of any individual or group. There are many people who look East Indian but have no such ancestry or cultural background. Some Middle Easterners have been mistaken for Puerto Ricans and vice versa. Some Arabs have been mistaken for black Americans, and so have many peoples from the tropical islands of the South Pacific. Biophysical traits should never be used as part of the definition of ethnicity. Every American should understand this explicitly, since there are millions of physically varying people, all sharing "American culture" (ethnicity), who know little or nothing about the cultural features of their ancestors, who may have arrived here from almost anywhere.

One of the tragedies of the racial worldview is that certain differences in physical appearance (especially among blacks and whites), the insignia of *race,* are so powerful as social dividers and status markers among Americans that they cannot perceive the cultural similarities that mark them all as Americans to outsiders. Europeans and Asians, however, not only tend to recognize these similarities but to treat such persons as part of a single ethnic American category. Michael Banton (1988) noted that in studies of children of nursery school age in Sweden, children were classified according to their home languages. This resulted in some African children being classified and referred to as Swedish, a much more realistic cognition of identity than skin color. Speaking the Swedish language reflects their participation in and acquaintance with Swedish culture, a fact that distinguishes them from foreigners who do not know the language or culture. Fourth- or fifth-generation Chinese and Japanese Americans who do not speak an Asian language or maintain elements of an Asian culture resent being mistaken for recent immigrants who have little experience and knowledge of American culture. One would think that Americans, of all people, would understand the power of enculturation and the rapidity with which ethnic characteristics and consciousness can change. But the force of the racial worldview prevents the cognitive acceptance of their implications.

Ethnic differences, interests, and identity are probably nearly as old as the human species, and so is ethnocentrism. Except for systems of supernatural belief and prohibitions against incest, few things are as universal in human societies as the penchant for dichotomizing their worlds into "we" and "they." That *our* customs, *our* laws, *our* food, *our* traditions, *our* music, *our* religion, *our* beliefs and values, and so forth are superior to or somehow better than those of other societies has been a widespread, and perhaps useful, construct for many groups. Ethnocentrism has varying manifestations, intensities, and consequences; although it may often convey an element of rivalry, it need not be accompanied by hostility. But nations and segments of modern nationstates reveal the greatest ethnocentric behavior when they are rivals for territory, resources, political hegemony, markets, souls, and so forth. Such rivalry may erupt into physical hostilities, or it maybe expressed in some other, nonlethal form. It may appear abruptly and diminish just as rapidly, or it may smolder for decades, generations, or even centuries, influencing the long-range interactions of both peoples. The important point about all cases of ethnocentrism is that it is grounded in the empirical reality and perceptions of sociocultural differences and the separateness of interests and goals that this may entail. There could be no ethnocentrism without cultural differences, no matter how trivial or insignificant these may appear to an outsider. (Consider the Walloons and Flemish, the Ibos and Yorubas, the Protestants and Catholics in Ireland, the Irish and English, the Basques and Spanish, the English and Germans, the Turks and Armenians, the Serbs and Croats, and dozens of other historical conflicts.)

Many situations reveal the most significant aspects of ethnocentrism, that is, its fluidity or flexibility and its potential transience. In the 1940s most Americans had hostile feelings toward the Germans and the Japanese. This attitude and the feelings it engendered changed in less than a generation. The transformation had nothing to do with alterations in our genetic structure. Values, attitudes, and beliefs are cultural traits and are nongenetic; they are extrasomatic, learned, and transmitted through enculturation processes. Individuals and groups can and do change their ethnic or cultural identities and interests through such processes as migration, conversion, and assimilation, or through exposure to other modifying influences.

Racism, on the other hand, does not require the presence of empirically determinable cultural differences. It substitutes, as it were, a fiction and a mystique about human behavior for the objective realization of true similarities and differences of language, religion, and other aspects of culture. This mystique is bound up with biological heredity and a belief in its ineradicable bonding to moral, spiritual, intellectual, and other mental and behavioral qualities. The mystique itself is the presumption of cultural-behavioral differences that phenotypic or physical differences are thought to signify. It is a belief in the biological determinants of cultural behavior—a critical ideological component of the concept of race.

But because phenotypic differences in a heterogeneous society can become muddled and confused (human mating habits not being thoroughly subject to coercion), and because the realities of true cultural similarities and differences sometimes penetrate its consciousness, a society predicated on race categories has to construct another fiction. This is the phenomenon of "racial essence," which is seen as the ultimate determinant of racial character and identity. The belief that an African American, for example, who appears phenotypically "white" (think ex-congressman Harold Ford or TV newscaster Soledad O'Brian) carries the racial essence of his or her black ancestors maintains the illusion of difference, distinctiveness, and innateness even without visible physical signs.

Race signifies rigidity and permanence of position and status within a ranking order that is based on what is believed to be the unalterable reality of innate biological differences. Ethnicity is conditional, temporal, even volitional, and not amenable to biology or biological processes. That some biophysical and ethnic (cultural) differences have coincided in the past (and still do) for largely geographical, ecological (adaptive), and historical reasons should not be permitted to confuse us. Nor should the fact that extreme ethnocentrism and race hatred often manifest some of the same symptoms. They can, and often do, accompany and complement each other, along with stereotypes that appear unabashedly racist. But ethnic stereotypes and ethnic boundaries can and do change, and much more rapidly than racial ones; ethnicity is based on behavior that most people understand can be learned.

Where race is the more powerful divider, it does not matter what one's sociocultural background may be or how similar ethnically two so-called racial groups are. In fact, the reality of ethnic, or social class, similarities and differences is irrelevant in situations where race is the prime and irreducible factor for social differentiation. The best example of this is blacks and whites in America, whose cultural similarities are so obvious to outsiders but internally are obfuscated by the racial worldview.

When the racial worldview is operant, an individual's or group's status can never alter, as both status and behavior are presumed to be biologically fixed. Stephen Steinberg captured this reality clearly in his discussion of ethnic (European) immigrants and racial minorities. "Immigrants," he observes, "were disparaged for their cultural peculiarities, and the implied message was, 'You will become like us whether you want to or not.' When it came to racial minorities, however, the unspoken dictum was, 'No matter how much like us you are, you will remain apart'" (1989, 42). The ideology of exclusion and low-status ranking for blacks in America precludes recognition of how culturally similar whites and blacks are. This is particularly true in the southern states where, class differences aside, they have shared a common culture for centuries.

Where ethnocentrism governs, a people's biophysical characteristics, no matter how similar or divergent, are immaterial to the sociocultural realities. What obtained in most of human history, and certainly throughout the ancient world, was an unarticulated understanding of these principles. This explains why so little was mentioned in ancient texts about the physical features of various groups. The ancients knew that differences of language and custom were far more significant than mere physical traits. They also knew, despite many statements that appear to us as "racist" (in some of the works of Tacitus and Herodotus, for example), that a German tribesman, or any other "barbarian" on the outskirts of civilization, could learn the language and culture of Romans and become a citizen—in other words, that the ethnicity of a person or group was not something inborn and irredeemable; it could be transformed.

But the modern world, after the great migrations of Europeans and the intermixtures among them and with non-Europeans, experienced disorder and confusion of class and ethnicity that crumbled old patterns of social identity and division. It was in large part the uncertainties of this situation that made the idea of race acceptable and useful. Indeed, it can be argued that, beginning in the nineteenth century, many differences that were once essentially ethnic in nature and origin have become transformed and expressed in a racial idiom. Race, because its characteristics are thought to be innate, exaggerates whatever differences do exist and renders them even more profound and permanent. Thus, race structures a social order that is perceived as unalterable.

Although the 1960s and 1970s brought a resurgence of ethnic consciousness and the application of the term "ethnic group" to blacks and other groups, Ronald Takaki has shown that Americans have historically treated ethnic and racial groups very differently. He concludes from a study of the political status of different groups that "what actually developed . . . in American society was a pattern of citizenship and suffrage which drew a very sharp distinction between 'ethnicity' and 'race' " (1987, 29). He argues that it is erroneous to treat subordinate racial groups in American society as if they were merely ethnic. Race is a qualitatively different mode of structuring society.

Race represents a systematic worldview that has proved useful to some people in situations of conflict and competition. It provides its own rationalization for the instigation and perpetuation of intergroup animosities and reduces or eliminates any potential for recognizing commonalities or reaching compromise. It evolved in the Judeo-Christian world as a justification for perpetrating inhumanities on others. Perhaps this is why so many people are made uncomfortable by its persistence. We can achieve a greater level of understanding of this phenomenon by examining how it was molded as an idea and an ideology throughout history.

References

Compare Banton 1977; Harris 1968; Montagu 1969; Stanton 1960; Van den Berghe 1967; and Williams [1944] 1966.

See Lewis 1971, 1990; Brown 1968; Davis 1984; and Hunwick 1978 for different perspectives on this topic.

See also Degler's strange argument regarding Brazilian "racial" feelings, especially where he assumes that negative attitudes toward darker-skinned (negroid) peoples who form much of the lower classes is due to a "universality of prejudice where there are visible differences among peoples" (1971, 287). Some writers who look at ancient documents immediately assume a racial element wherever they see negative descriptions or derogatory comments about the physical characteristics of an alien people. Were we to accept such a wide view of race, virtually all relationships among human groups would involve some form of racial belief, and we would not be able to refine this definition so that comparative studies could be made.

St. Clair Drake made a similar distinction between color prejudice and racism (1987, 8–10). Many cultures place social meanings on differences in skin color that have nothing to do with race. In Japanese history, women with pale skins were aesthetically highly valued, in part because this skin tone signaled that their fathers (or husbands) were wealthy and the women therefore did not need to work outside in the fields (Wagatsuma 1968). In contrast, white Americans often acquire deep tans to convey an aura of affluence, high status, and leisure. Drake also believed that, among other factors, negative aesthetic evaluations of negroid physiognomy affected attitudes toward Africans in many societies quite apart from mere skin color preferences or prejudices. But aesthetic values are subjective and highly personal. One would be hard-pressed to identify the kind of evidence needed to prove this.

See Frank Snowden's description of blacks in ancient Greek and Roman societies ([1970] 1983).

This definition is frequently quoted in introductory textbooks in anthropology. See, for example, Harris, 1995, 7; Swartz and Jordan 1976, 4; and Keesing and Keesing 1971, 20, among many others.

Questions for Discussion

1. Why is the chapter entitled "Race as a Worldview"?

2. What were the "five ingredients" of a racial worldview in the United States during the 1800s?

3. Which of these five elements still exist today? Give specific examples of how each is no longer important or is still a strong factor in US society.

4. Why was it important for people to believe that the "ranking" or "hierarchy" of superior and inferior races was "natural" or a "God given order"?

5. Name at least five historical events between 1850 and 1950 that either encouraged a "racial worldview" or moved Americans toward an "antiracist worldview" and explain how "race" was a key factor in these events.

6. What does it mean to be a member of an "ethnic group"? How are *race/racism* and *ethnicity/ ethnocentrism* similar or different from one another? Give examples of ethnic conflicts based on "ethnocentrism" outside or within the United States.

7. Smedley and Smedley state that in Sweden, anyone who speaks Swedish is treated as a member of Swedish society, as distinguished from "foreigners" who do not know about Swedish culture and language. Does "being American" over two or more generations have the same outcome? Why or why not?

8. The "one drop rule" is based on both social and legal rules and laws about "race" in the United States. How has this been an example of what the Smedleys call "racial essence"?

9. Why is "race" a stronger social divider than "ethnicity"? For example, what did Dr. Ronald Takaki mean when he stated that "what actually developed . . . in American society was a pattern of citizenship and suffrage which drew a very sharp contrast between 'ethnicity' and 'race' "?

CHAPTER 2

Replenishing Mexican Ethnicity

Thomas R. Jimenez

Mexican Americans' structural assimilation and the intergenerational decline of ethnic traditions and customs within the family do not lead to a purely symbolic form of ethnic identity, as canonical theories of assimilation predict. Instead, immigrant replenishment provides a sun that staves off the twilight of ethnicity among later-generation Mexican Americans. The large Mexican-immigrant and second-generation populations have made Mexican ethnicity a prominent part of the social structure in these two cities, and ethnicity is a more accessible and salient aspect of Mexican Americans' social identity as a result.

The social "construction" of racial and ethnic categories and their corresponding identities is virtually taken for granted; these are not biological or "natural" aspects of social life. Rather, they result from human interaction and are shaped by social, political, and economic processes. Much of the recent theorizing of race and ethnicity has focused on the social construction of the boundaries that define groups and that enclose the "ethnic stuff" commonly referred to as culture. Scholars have illuminated the ways in which boundaries shift and are crossed and blurred (Alba 2005b; Alba and Nee 2003), the varying character and consequences of ethnic boundaries (Wimmer 2008b), as well as the ways in which individuals change ethnic boundaries (Wimmer 2008a). Boundaries are indeed important for understanding racial and ethnic changes, but we cannot fully understand ethnic identity by focusing exclusively on boundaries. The expression of ethnic culture—art, music, food, language, style of dress, holidays, and so forth—is also central to the construction of ethnic identity. Ethnic boundaries and the culture they enclose are two sides of the ethnic coin; thus, considering both the cultural content of ethnicity and the ethnic boundaries that delineates groups is important. As sociologist Joane Nagel notes, culture "provides the content and meaning of ethnicity; it animates and authenticates ethnic boundaries by providing a history, ideology, symbolic universe, and system of meaning. Culture answers the question: What are we?" (1997, 162). In this chapter I examine how ongoing Mexican immigration shapes Mexican Americans' answer to this question, by focusing on how Mexican Americans express their ethnic identity. In chapter 5 I turn to the other side of the ethnic coin by exploring how immigrant replenishment shapes ethnic boundaries.

If racial and ethnic identities are constructed (and I argue that they are), then the strength of attachment that people have to an identity rooted in ethnicity depends in large part on the availability of ethnically linked resources for their construction of that identity. As Richard Alba notes, "Groups that have a greater supply of cultural resources provide their, members with more material to stimulate a sense of identity. Conversely these groups also depend on that sense of identity; without it, the critical mass necessary to maintain the ethnic cultural supply would dissipate" (1990, 121). The cultural resources to which Alba refers can be thought of as "ethnic raw materials"—ethnically linked symbols and practices—that are necessary for the construction of a salient ethnic identity. If ethnic raw materials are lacking, then ethnic identity takes on a purely symbolic form and is not well integrated into an individual's overall identity. But if ethnic raw materials are in abundant supply, then the possibility of constructing an ethnic identity that is more central to an individual's identity increases. The experience of Mexican Americans shows that even if the ethnic raw materials are not passed down from the immigrant generation to the later generations within the family, Mexican immigration provides ample ethnic raw materials that help Mexican Americans construct an ethnic identity that is more central to their overall identity.

This chapter explains both the micro- and macroprocesses through which Mexican immigration provides Mexican Americans opportunities to engage in the practice of ethnicity. It shows how opportunities to access ethnic raw materials ultimately contributed to a more salient ethnic identity for the people I interviewed. Everyday interactions with Mexican immigrants and second-generation Mexican Americans allowed respondents abundant access to the symbols and practices associated with Mexican ethnicity. The presence of a large Mexican-immigrant population also provided more abundant and more frequent opportunities for them to feel connected to an ethnic identity through ethnicity's infusion into religion, civic organizations, mass media, and the cuisine that Mexican Americans access.

More than just demographic shifts act on Mexican Americans' ethnic identity. Larger ideological changes have made ethnicity a more desirable aspect of social identity. Long gone are the days when Americanization stood as the dominant ideology guiding nonwhites' forced homogenization. Instead, Americanization now stands alongside the formidable ideological contender of multiculturalism, which values, however superficially in some cases, a strong connection to one's ethnic origins. This multicultural ideology helps lift the stigma placed on Mexican ethnicity, making it a desirable and even a rewarding aspect of identity for Mexican Americans.

Mexican Immigration and Ethnic Raw Materials in the Social Structure

The social structure in which Mexican Americans are embedded is replete with a Mexican-immigrant population that provides them with abundant opportunities to engage in the practice of ethnicity. Casual contact with Mexican immigrants in public spaces and in the workplace primarily strengthens Mexican Americans' ability to speak Spanish, and friendships and romantic relationships with immigrants and the second generation bring opportunities for Mexican Americans to engage in an array of ethnic practices closer to home. These relationships exposed the people I interviewed to holidays, cuisine, and other ties to Mexico that would not have existed had it not been for a large Mexican-immigrant population. Mexican Americans need not have direct interaction with immigrants to experience greater exposure to Mexican ethnicity. Immigration from their ethnic homeland injects heavy doses of ethnicity into the broader community, including churches, schools, restaurants, grocery stores, and mass media, providing Mexican Americans opportunities to partake in ethnically linked practices that make ethnicity more central to their identity.

CHAPTER 3

Racial Formation in the United States: From the 1960s to the 1980s

Michael Omi and Howard Winant

Race as a Social Concept

The social sciences have come to reject biologistic notions of race in favor of an approach which regards race as a *social* concept. Beginning in the eighteenth century, this trend has been slow and uneven, but its direction is clear. In the nineteenth century Max Weber discounted biological explanations for racial conflict and instead highlighted the social and political factors which engendered such conflict. The work of pioneering cultural anthropologist Franz Boas was crucial in refuting the scientific racism of the early twentieth century by rejecting the connection between race and culture, and the assumption of a continuum of "higher" and "lower" cultural groups. Within the contemporary social science literature, race is assumed to be a variable which is shaped by broader societal forces.

Race is indeed a preeminently *sociohistorical* concept. Racial categories and the meaning of race are given concrete expression by the specific social relations and historical context in which they are embedded. Racial meanings have varied tremendously over time and between different societies.

In the United States, the black/white color line has historically been rigidly defined and enforced. White is seen as a "pure" category. Any racial intermixture makes one "nonwhite." In the movie *Raintree County,* Elizabeth Taylor describes the worst of fates to befall whites as "havin' a little Negra blood in ya'—just one little teeny drop and a person's all Negra." This thinking flows from what Marvin Harris has characterized as the principle of *hypo-descent:*

> By what ingenious computation is the genetic tracery of a million years of evolution unraveled and each man [sic] assigned his proper social box? In the United States, the mechanism employed is the rule of hypo-descent. This descent rule requires Americans to believe that anyone who is known to have had a Negro ancestor is a Negro. We admit nothing in between. . . . "Hypo-descent" means affiliation with the subordinate rather than the superordinate group in order to avoid the ambiguity of intermediate identity. . . . The rule of hypo-descent is, therefore, an invention, which we in the United States have made in order to keep biological facts from intruding into our collective racist fantasies.

The Susie Guillory Phipps case merely represents the contemporary expression of this racial logic.

By contrast, a striking feature of race relations in the lowland areas of Latin America since the abolition of slavery has been the relative absence of sharply defined racial groupings. No such rigid descent rule characterizes racial identity in many Latin American societies. Brazil, for example, has historically had less rigid conceptions of race, and thus a variety of "intermediate" racial categories exist. Indeed, as Harris notes, "One of the most striking consequences of the Brazilian system of racial identification is that parents and children and even brothers and sisters are frequently accepted as representatives of quite opposite racial types." Such a possibility is incomprehensible within the logic of racial categories in the United States.

To suggest another example, the notion of "passing" takes on new meaning if we compare various American cultures' means of assigning racial identity. In the United States, individuals who are actually "black" by the logic of hypo-descent have attempted to skirt the discriminatory barriers imposed by law and custom by attempting to "pass" for white. Ironically, these same individuals would not be able to pass for "black" in many Latin American societies.

Consideration of the term "black" illustrates the diversity of racial meanings which can be found among different societies and historically within a given society. In contemporary British politics the term "black" is used to refer to all nonwhites. Interestingly this designation has not arisen through the racist discourse of groups such as the National Front. Rather, in political and cultural movements, Asian as well as Afro-Caribbean youth are adopting the term as an expression of self-identity. The wide-ranging meanings of "black" illustrate the manner in which racial categories are shaped politically.

The meaning of race is defined and contested throughout society, in both collective action and personal practice. In the process, racial categories themselves are formed, transformed, destroyed, and re-formed. We use the term *racial formation* to refer to the process by which social, economic, and political forces determine the content and importance of racial categories, and by which they are in turn shaped by racial meanings. Crucial to this formulation is the treatment of race as a *central axis* of social relations which cannot be subsumed under or reduced to some broader category or conception.

Racial Ideology and Racial Identity

The seemingly obvious, "natural" and "common sense" qualities which the existing racial order exhibits themselves testify to the effectiveness of the racial formation process in constructing racial meanings and racial identities.

One of the first things we notice about people when we meet them (along with their sex) is their race. We utilize race to provide clues about *who* a person is. This fact is made painfully obvious when we encounter someone whom we cannot conveniently racially categorize—someone who is, for example, racially "mixed" or of an ethnic/racial group with which we are not familiar. Such an encounter becomes a source of discomfort and momentarily a crisis of racial meaning. Without a racial identity, one is in danger of having no identity.

Our compass for navigating race relations depends on preconceived notions of what each specific racial group looks like. Comments such as, "Funny, you don't look black," betray an underlying image of what black should be. We also become disoriented when people do not act "black," "Latino," or indeed "white." The content of such stereotypes reveals a series of unsubstantiated beliefs about who these groups are and what "they" are like.

In US society, then, a kind of "racial etiquette" exists, a set of interpretative codes and racial meanings which operate in the interactions of daily life. Rules shaped by our perception of race in a comprehensively racial society determine the "presentation of self," distinctions of status, and appropriate modes of conduct. "Etiquette" is not mere universal adherence to the dominant group's rules, but a more dynamic combination of these rules with the values and beliefs of subordinated groupings. This racial "subjection" is quintessentially ideological. Everybody learns some combination, some version, of the rules of racial classification, and of their own racial identity, often without obvious teaching or conscious inculcation. Race becomes "common sense"—a way of comprehending, explaining, and acting in the world.

Racial beliefs operate as an "amateur biology," a way of explaining the variations in "human nature." Differences in skin color and other obvious physical characteristics supposedly provide visible clues to differences lurking underneath. Temperament, sexuality, intelligence, athletic ability, aesthetic preferences, and so on are presumed to be fixed and discernible from the palpable mark of race. Such diverse questions as our confidence and trust in others (for example, clerks or salespeople, media figures, neighbors), our sexual preferences and romantic images, our tastes in music, films, dance, or sports, and our very ways of talking, walking, eating, and dreaming are ineluctably shaped by notions of race. Skin color "differences" are thought to explain perceived differences in intellectual, physical, and artistic temperaments and to justify distinct treatment of racially identified individuals and groups.

The continuing persistence of racial ideology suggests that these racial myths and stereotypes cannot be exposed as such in the popular imagination. They are, we think, too essential, too integral, to the maintenance of the US social order. Of course, particular meanings, stereotypes, and myths can change, but the presence of a *system* of racial meanings and stereotypes, of racial ideology, seems to be a permanent feature of US culture.

Film and television, for example, have been notorious in disseminating images of racial minorities which establish for audiences what people from these groups look like, how they behave, and "who they are." The power of the media lies not only in their ability to reflect the dominant racial ideology, but in their capacity to shape that ideology in the first place. D. W. Griffith's epic *Birth of a Nation,* a sympathetic treatment of the rise of the Ku Klux Klan during Reconstruction, helped to generate, consolidate, and "nationalize" images of blacks which had been more disparate (more regionally specific, for example) prior to the film's appearance. In US television, the necessity to define characters in the briefest and most condensed manner has led to the perpetuation of racial caricatures, as racial stereotypes serve as shorthand for scriptwriters, directors and actors, in commercials, etc. Television's tendency to address the "lowest common denominator" in order to render programs "familiar" to an enormous and diverse audience leads it regularly to assign and reassign racial characteristics to particular groups, both minority and majority.

These and innumerable other examples show that we tend to view race as something fixed and immutable—something rooted in "nature." Thus we mask the historical construction of racial categories, the shifting meaning of race, and the crucial role of politics and ideology in shaping race relations. Races do not emerge full-blown. They are the results of diverse historical practices and are continually subject to challenge over their definition and meaning.

Racialization: The Historical Development of Race

In the United States, the racial category of "black" evolved with the consolidation of racial slavery. By the end of the seventeenth century, Africans whose specific identity was Ibo, Yoruba, Fulani, etc., were rendered "black" by an ideology of exploitation based on racial logic—the establishment and maintenance of a "color line." This of course did not occur overnight. A period of indentured servitude which was not rooted in racial logic preceded the consolidation of racial slavery. With slavery, however, a racially based understanding of society was set in motion which resulted in the shaping of a specific *racial* identity not only for the slaves but for the European settlers as well. Winthrop Jordan has observed: "From the initially common term *Christian,* at mid-century there was a marked shift toward the terms *English* and *free.* After about 1680, taking the colonies as a whole, a new term of self-identification appeared—*white.*"

We employ the term *racialization* to signify the extension of racial meaning to a previously racially unclassified relationship, social practice, or group. Racialization is an ideological process, an historically specific one. Racial ideology is constructed from preexisting conceptual (or, if one prefers, "discursive") elements and emerges from the struggles of competing political projects and ideas seeking to articulate similar elements differently. An account of racialization processes that avoids the pitfalls of US ethnic history remains to be written.

Particularly during the nineteenth century, the category of "white" was subject to challenges brought about by the influx of diverse groups who were not of the same Anglo-Saxon stock as the founding immigrants. In the nineteenth century, political and ideological struggles emerged over the classification of Southern Europeans, the Irish and Jews, among other "nonwhite" categories. Nativism was only effectively curbed by the institutionalization of a racial order that drew the color line *around,* rather than *within,* Europe.

By stopping short of racializing immigrants from Europe after the Civil War, and by subsequently allowing their assimilation, the American racial order was reconsolidated in the wake of the tremendous challenge placed before it by the abolition of racial slavery. With the end of Reconstruction in 1877, an effective program for limiting the emergent class struggles of the later nineteenth century was forged: the definition of the working class *in racial terms*—as "white." This was not accomplished by any legislative decree or capitalist maneuvering to divide the working class, but rather by white workers themselves. Many of them were recent immigrants, who organized on racial lines as much as on traditionally defined class lines. The Irish on the West Coast, for example, engaged in vicious anti-Chinese race-baiting and committed many pogrom-type assaults on Chinese in the course of consolidating the trade union movement in California.

Thus the very political organization of the working class was in important ways a racial project. The legacy of racial conflicts and arrangements shaped the definition of interests and in turn led to the consolidation of institutional patterns (for example, segregated unions, dual labor markets, exclusionary legislation) which perpetuated the color line *within* the working class. Selig Perlman, whose study of the development of the labor movement is fairly sympathetic to this process, notes that:

> The political issue after 1877 was racial, not financial, and the weapon was not merely the ballot, but also "direct action"—violence. The anti-Chinese agitation in California, culminating as it did in the Exclusion Law passed by Congress in 1882, was doubtless the most important single factor in the history of American labor, for without it the entire country might have been overrun by Mongolian [sic] labor and *the labor movement might have become a conflict of races instead of one of classes.*

More recent economic transformations in the United States have also altered interpretations of racial identities and meanings. The automation of southern agriculture and the augmented labor demand of the postwar boom transformed blacks from a largely rural, impoverished labor force to a largely urban, working-class group by 1970. When boom became bust and liberal welfare statism moved rightwards, the majority of blacks came to be seen, increasingly, as part of the "underclass," as state "dependents." Thus the particularly deleterious effects on blacks of global and national economic shifts (generally rising unemployment rates, changes in the employment structure away from reliance on labor intensive work, etc.) were explained once again in the late 1970s and 1980s (as they had been in the 1940s and mid-1960s) as the result of defective black cultural norms, of familial disorganization, etc. In this way new racial attributions, new racial myths, are affixed to "blacks." Similar changes in racial identity are presently affecting Asians and Latinos, as such economic forces as increasing Third World impoverishment and indebtedness fuel immigration and high interest rates, Japanese competition spurs resentments, and US jobs seem to fly away to Korea and Singapore.

Questions for Discussion

1. Why do sociologists Omi & Winant open their book with the story of Susie Phipps? What does her story tell us about the idea of "race" as explained by anthropologists Smedley & Smedley in our readings?

2. If "race" is not just a matter of appearance or skin color, than what is it? Why does it matter in the past and present of the United States?

3. What do Omi & Winant mean when they suggest that we think about "race as an element of social structure rather than as an irregularity within it"?

4. According to Omi & Winant, is "prejudice" a cause or an effect of injustice and racial inequality? EXPLAIN.

5. Does "discrimination" occur because of individual actions based on personal prejudice or because of intentional policies to deny people access to resources based on their "race"? EXPLAIN WHAT THEY MEAN BY RACISM AS A "STRUCTURAL FEATURE" OF U.S. SOCIETY.

6. What are the two views about "racism" that have evolved in the United States since the 1960s and 1970s ("institutionalized" or "color-blind")?

7. What do the authors mean by "racial formation" and "noticing" race as alternative ways of thinking about "race" and overcoming racism?

CHAPTER 4

Why Are All the Black Kids Sitting Together in the Cafeteria?: And Other Conversations About Race

Beverly Daniel Tatum, Ph.D.

Defining Racism

"Can we talk?"

Early in my teaching career, a White student I knew asked me what I would be teaching the following semester. I mentioned that I would be teaching a course on racism. She replied, with some surprise in her voice, "Oh, is there still racism?" I assured her that indeed there was and suggested that she sign up for my course. Fifteen years later, after exhaustive media coverage of events such as the Rodney King beating, the Charles Stuart and Susan Smith cases, the O. J. Simpson trial, the appeal to racial prejudices in electoral politics, and the bitter debates about affirmative action and welfare reform, it seems hard to imagine that anyone would still be unaware of the reality of racism in our society. But in fact, in almost every audience I address, there is someone who will suggest that racism is a thing of the past. There is always someone who hasn't noticed the stereotypical images of people of color in the media, who hasn't observed the housing discrimination in their community, who hasn't read the newspaper articles about documented racial bias in lending practices among well-known banks, who isn't aware of the racial tracking pattern at the local school, who hasn't seen the reports of rising incidents of racially motivated hate crimes in America—in short, someone who hasn't been paying attention to issues of race. But if you are paying attention, the legacy of racism is not hard to see, and we are all affected by it.

The impact of racism begins early. Even in our preschool years, we are exposed to misinformation about people different from ourselves. Many of us grew up in neighborhoods where we had limited opportunities to interact with people different from our own families.

When I ask my college students, "How many of you grew up in neighborhoods where most of the people were from the same racial group as your own?" almost every hand goes up. There is still a great deal of social segregation in our communities. Consequently, most of the early information we receive about "others"—people racially, religiously, or socioeconomically different from ourselves—does not come as the result of firsthand experience. The secondhand information we do receive has often been distorted, shaped by cultural stereotypes, and left incomplete.

Some examples will highlight this process. Several years ago one of my students conducted a research project investigating preschoolers' conceptions of Native Americans. Using children at a local day care center as her participants, she asked these three- and four-year-olds to draw a picture of a Native American. Most children were stumped by her request. They didn't know what a Native American was. But when she rephrased the question and asked them to draw a picture of an Indian, they readily complied. Almost every picture included one central feature: feathers. In fact, many of them also included a weapon—a knife or tomahawk—and depicted the person in violent or aggressive terms. Though this group of children, almost all of whom were White, did not live near a large Native American population and probably had had little if any personal interaction with American Indians, they all had internalized an image of what Indians were like. How did they know? Cartoon images, in particular the Disney movie *Peter Pan,* were cited by the children as their number-one source of information. At the age of three, these children already had a set of stereotypes in place. Though I would not describe three-year-olds as prejudiced, the stereotypes to which they have been exposed become the foundation for the adult prejudices so many of us have.

Sometimes the assumptions we make about others come not from what we have been told or what we have seen on television or in books, but rather from what we have *not* been told. The distortion of historical information about people of color leads young people (and older people, too) to make assumptions that may go unchallenged for a long time. Consider this conversation between two White students following a discussion about the cultural transmission of racism:

"Yeah, I just found out that Cleopatra was actually a Black woman."
"What?"

The first student went on to explain her newly learned information. The second student exclaimed in disbelief, "That can't be true. Cleopatra was beautiful!"

What had this young woman learned about who in our society is considered beautiful and who is not? Had she conjured up images of Elizabeth Taylor when she thought of Cleopatra? The new information her classmate had shared and her own deeply ingrained assumptions about who is beautiful and who is not were too incongruous to allow her to assimilate the information at that moment.

Omitted information can have similar effects. For example, another young woman, preparing to be a high school English teacher, expressed her dismay that she had never learned about any Black authors in any of her English courses. How was she to teach about them to her future students when she hadn't learned about them herself? A White male student in the class responded to this discussion with frustration in his response journal, writing "It's not my fault that Blacks don't write books." Had one of his elementary, high school, or college teachers ever told him that there were no Black writers? Probably not. Yet because he had never been exposed to Black authors, he had drawn his own conclusion that there were none.

Stereotypes, omissions, and distortions all contribute to the development of prejudice. *Prejudice* is a preconceived judgment or opinion, usually based on limited information. I assume that we all have prejudices, not because we want them, but simply because we are so continually exposed to misinformation about others. Though I have often heard students or workshop participants describe someone as not having "a prejudiced bone in his body," I usually suggest that they look again. Prejudice is one of the inescapable consequences of living in a racist society. Cultural racism—the cultural images and messages that affirm the assumed superiority of Whites and the assumed inferiority of people of color—is like smog in the air. Sometimes it is so thick it is visible, other times it is less apparent, but always, day in and day out, we are breathing it in. None of us would introduce ourselves as "smog-breathers" (and most of us don't want to be described as prejudiced), but if we live in a smoggy place, how can we avoid breathing the air? If we live in an environment in which we are bombarded with stereotypical images in the media, are frequently exposed to the ethnic jokes of friends and family members, and are rarely informed of the accomplishments of oppressed groups, we will develop the negative categorizations of those groups that form the basis of prejudice.

People of color as well as Whites develop these categorizations. Even a member of the stereotyped group may internalize the stereotypical categories about his or her own group to some degree. In fact, this process happens so frequently that it has a name, *internalized oppression*. Some of the consequences of believing the distorted messages about one's own group will be discussed in subsequent chapters.

Certainly some people are more prejudiced than others, actively embracing and perpetuating negative and hateful images of those who are different from themselves. When we claim to be free of prejudice, perhaps what we are really saying is that we are not hate-mongers. But none of us is completely innocent. Prejudice is an integral part of our socialization, and it is not our fault. Just as the preschoolers my student interviewed are not to blame for the negative messages they internalized, we are not at fault for the stereotypes, distortions, and omissions that shaped our thinking as we grew up.

To say that it is not our fault does not relieve us of responsibility, however. We may not have polluted the air, but we need to take responsibility, along with others, for cleaning it up. Each of us needs to look at our own behavior. Am I perpetuating and reinforcing the negative messages so pervasive in our culture, or am I seeking to challenge them? If I have not been exposed to positive images of marginalized groups, am I seeking them out, expanding my own knowledge base for myself and my children? Am I acknowledging and examining my own prejudices, my own rigid categorizations of others, thereby minimizing the adverse impact they might have on my interactions with those I have categorized? Unless we engage in these and other conscious acts of reflection and reeducation, we easily repeat the process with our children. We teach what we were taught. The unexamined prejudices of the parents are passed on to the children. It is not our fault, but it is our responsibility to interrupt this cycle.

Racism: A System of Advantage Based on Race

Many people use the terms *prejudice* and *racism* interchangeably. I do not, and I think it is important to make a distinction. In his book *Portraits of White Racism,* David Wellman argues convincingly that limiting our understanding of racism to prejudice does not offer a sufficient explanation for the persistence of racism. He defines racism as a "system of advantage based on race." In illustrating this definition, he provides example after example of how Whites defend their racial advantage—access to better schools, housing, jobs—even when they do not embrace overtly prejudicial thinking. Racism cannot be fully explained as an expression of prejudice alone.

This definition of racism is useful because it allows us to see that racism, like other forms of oppression, is not only a personal ideology based on racial prejudice, but a *system* involving cultural messages and institutional policies and practices as well as the beliefs and actions of individuals. In the context of the United States, this system clearly operates to the advantage of Whites and to the disadvantage of people of color. Another related definition of racism, commonly used by antiracist educators and consultants, is "prejudice plus power." Racial prejudice when combined with social power—access to social, cultural, and economic resources and decision making—leads to the institutionalization of racist policies and practices. While I think this definition also captures the idea that racism is more than individual beliefs and attitudes, I prefer Wellman's definition because the idea of systematic advantage and disadvantage is critical to an understanding of how racism operates in American society.

In addition, I find that many of my White students and workshop participants do not feel powerful. Defining racism as prejudice plus power has little personal relevance. For some, their response to this definition is the following: "I'm not really prejudiced, and I have no power, so racism has nothing to do with me." However, most White people, if they are really being honest with themselves, can see that there are advantages to being White in the United States. Despite the current rhetoric about affirmative action and "reverse racism," every social indicator, from salary to life expectancy, reveals the advantages of being White.

The systematic advantages of being White are often referred to as White privilege. In a now well-known article, "White Privilege: Unpacking the Invisible Knapsack," Peggy McIntosh, a White feminist scholar, identified a long list of societal privileges that she received simply because she was White. She did not ask for them, and it is important to note that she hadn't always noticed that she was receiving them. They included major and minor advantages. Of course she enjoyed greater access to jobs and housing. But she also was able to shop in department stores without being followed by suspicious salespeople and could always find appropriate hair care products and makeup in any drugstore. She could send her child to school confident that the teacher would not discriminate against him on the basis of race. She could also be late for meetings, and talk with her mouth full, fairly confident that these behaviors would not be attributed to the fact that she was White. She could express an opinion in a meeting or in print and not have it labeled the "White" viewpoint. In other words, she was more often than not viewed as an individual, rather than as a member of a racial group.

This article rings true for most White readers, many of whom may have never considered the benefits of being White. It's one thing to have enough awareness of racism to describe the ways that people of color are disadvantaged by it. But this new understanding of racism is more elusive. In very concrete terms, it means that if a person of color is the victim of housing discrimination, the apartment that would otherwise have been rented to that person of color is still available for a White person. The White tenant is, knowingly or unknowingly, the beneficiary of racism, a system of advantage based on race. The unsuspecting tenant is not to blame for the prior discrimination, but she benefits from it anyway.

For many Whites, this new awareness of the benefits of a racist system elicits considerable pain, often accompanied by feelings of anger and guilt. These uncomfortable emotions can hinder further discussion. We all like to think that we deserve the good things we have received, and that others, too, get what they deserve. Social psychologists call this tendency a "belief in a just world." Racism directly contradicts such notions of justice.

Understanding racism as a system of advantage based on race is antithetical to traditional notions of an American meritocracy. For those who have internalized this myth, this definition generates considerable discomfort. It is more comfortable simply to think of racism as a particular form of prejudice. Notions of power or privilege do not have to be addressed when our understanding of racism is constructed in that way.

The discomfort generated when a systemic definition of racism is introduced is usually quite visible in the workshops I lead. Someone in the group is usually quick to point out that this is not the definition you will find in most dictionaries. I reply, "Who wrote the dictionary?" I am not being facetious with this response. Whose interests are served by a "prejudice only" definition of racism? It is important to understand that the system of advantage is perpetuated when we do not acknowledge its existence.

On Tatum

Tatum discusses the difference between defining racism as prejudice and defining it as systemic advantage and disadvantage. Think about the history of race in America. Which definition is more useful in understanding the following events and institutions? That is, will we come to a fuller understanding of these events if we look for dynamics of individual prejudice, or systemic power relationships?

1. Dispossession of native lands
2. Slavery
3. Jim Crow
4. Chinese exclusion
5. Whites-only naturalization
6. Housing segregation
7. Unequal education
8. Unequal wealth distribution
9. Unequal political representation

Racism: For Whites Only?

Frequently someone will say, "You keep talking about White people. People of color can be racist, too." I once asked a White teacher what it would mean to her if a student or parent of color accused her of being racist. She said she would feel as though she had been punched in the stomach or called a "low-life scum." She is not alone in this feeling. The word *racist* holds a lot of emotional power. For many White people, to be called racist is the ultimate insult. The idea that this term might only be applied to Whites becomes highly problematic for after all, can't people of color be "low-life scum" too?

Of course, people of any racial group can hold hateful attitudes and behave in racially discriminatory and bigoted ways. We can all cite examples of horrible hate crimes which have been perpetrated by people of color as well as Whites. Hateful behavior is hateful behavior no matter who does it. But when I am asked, "Can people of color be racist?" I reply, "The answer depends on your definition of racism." If one defines racism as racial prejudice, the answer is yes. People of color can and do have racial prejudices. However, if one defines racism as a system of advantage based on race, the answer is no. People of color are not racist because they do not systematically benefit from racism. And equally important, there is no systematic cultural and institutional support or sanction for the racial bigotry of people of color. In my view, reserving the term *racist* only for behaviors committed by Whites in the context of a White-dominated society is a way of acknowledging the ever-present power differential afforded Whites by the culture and institutions that make up the system of advantage and continue to reinforce notions of White superiority. (Using the same logic, I reserve the word *sexist* for men. Though women can and do have gender-based prejudices, only men systematically benefit from sexism.)

Despite my best efforts to explain my thinking on this point, there are some who will be troubled, perhaps even incensed, by my response. To call the racially motivated acts of a person of color acts of racial bigotry and to describe similar acts committed by Whites as racist will make no sense to some people, including some people of color. To those, I will respectfully say, "We can agree to disagree." At moments like these, it is not agreement that is essential, but clarity. Even if you don't like the definition of racism I am using, hopefully you are now clear about what it is. If I also understand how you are using the term, our conversation can continue—despite our disagreement.

Another provocative question I'm often asked is "Are you saying all Whites are racist?" When asked this question, I again remember that White teacher's response, and I am conscious that perhaps the question I am really being asked is "Are you saying all Whites are bad people?" The answer to that question is of course not. However, all White people, intentionally or unintentionally, do benefit from racism. A more relevant question is what are White people as individuals doing to interrupt racism? For many White people, the image of a racist is a hood-wearing Klan member or a name-calling Archie Bunker figure. These images represent what might be called *active racism,* blatant, intentional acts of racial bigotry, and discrimination. *Passive racism* is more subtle and can be seen in the collusion of laughing when a racist joke is told, of letting exclusionary hiring practices go unchallenged, of accepting as appropriate the omissions of people of color from the curriculum, and of avoiding difficult race-related issues. Because racism is so ingrained in the fabric of American institutions, it is easily self-perpetuating. All that is required to maintain it is business as usual.

I sometimes visualize the ongoing cycle of racism as a moving walkway at the airport. Active racist behavior is equivalent to walking fast on the conveyor belt. The person engaged in active racist behavior has identified with the ideology of White supremacy and is moving with it. Passive racist behavior is equivalent to standing still on the walkway. No overt effort is being made, but the conveyor belt moves the bystanders along to the same destination as those who are actively walking. Some of the bystanders may feel the motion of the conveyor belt, see the active racists ahead of them, and choose to turn around, unwilling to go to the same destination as the White supremacists. But unless they are walking actively in the opposite direction at a speed faster than the conveyor belt—unless they are actively antiracist—they will find themselves carried along with the others.

So, not all Whites are actively racist. Many are passively racist. Some, though not enough, are actively antiracist. The relevant question is not whether all Whites are racist, but how we can move more White people from a position of active or passive racism to one of active antiracism? The task of interrupting racism is obviously not the task of Whites alone. But the fact of White privilege means that Whites have greater access to the societal institutions in need of transformation. To whom much is given, much is required.

It is important to acknowledge that while all Whites benefit from racism, they do not all benefit equally. Other factors, such as socioeconomic status, gender, age, religious affiliation, sexual orientation, and mental and physical ability, also play a role in our access to social influence and power. A White woman on welfare is not privileged to the same extent as a wealthy White heterosexual man. In her case, the systematic disadvantages of sexism and classism intersect with her White privilege, but the privilege is still there. This point was brought home to me in a 1994 study conducted by a Mount Holyoke graduate student, Phyllis Wentworth. Wentworth interviewed a group of female college students, who were both older than their peers and were the first members of their families to attend college, about the pathways that lead them to college. All of the women interviewed were White, from working-class backgrounds, from families where women were expected to graduate from high school and get married or get a job. Several had experienced abusive relationships and other personal difficulties prior to coming to college. Yet their experiences were punctuated by "good luck" stories of apartments obtained without a deposit, good jobs offered without experience or extensive reference checks, and encouragement provided by willing mentors. While the women acknowledged their good fortune, none of them discussed their Whiteness. They had not considered the possibility that being White had worked in their favor and helped give them the benefit of the doubt at critical junctures. This study clearly showed that even under difficult circumstances, White privilege was still operating.

It is also true that not all people of color are equally targeted by racism. We all have multiple identities that shape our experience. I can describe myself as a light-skinned, well-educated, heterosexual, able-bodied, Christian African American woman raised in a middle-class suburb. As an African American woman, I am systematically disadvantaged by race and by gender, but I systematically receive benefits in the other categories, which then mediate my experience of racism and sexism. When one is targeted by multiple isms—racism, sexism, classism, heterosexism, ableism, anti-Semitism, ageism—in whatever combination, the effect is intensified. The particular combination of racism and classism in many communities of color is life-threatening. Nonetheless, when I, the middle-class Black mother of two sons, read another story about a Black man's unlucky encounter with a White police officer's deadly force, I am reminded that racism by itself can kill.

The Cost of Racism

Several years ago, a White male student in my psychology of racism course wrote in his journal at the end of the semester that he had learned a lot about racism and now understood in a way he never had before just how advantaged he was. He also commented that he didn't think he would do anything to try to change the situation. After all, the system was working in his favor. Fortunately, his response was not typical. Most of my students leave my course with the desire (and an action plan) to interrupt the cycle of racism. However, this young man's response does raise an important question. Why should Whites who are advantaged by racism *want* to end that system of advantage? What are the *costs* of that system to them?

A *Money* magazine article called "Race and Money" chronicled the many ways the American economy was hindered by institutional racism. Whether one looks at productivity lowered by racial tensions in the workplace, or real estate equity lost through housing discrimination, or the tax revenue lost in underemployed communities of color, or the high cost of warehousing human talent in prison, the economic costs of racism are real and measurable.

As a psychologist, I often hear about the less easily measured costs. When I ask White men and women how racism hurts them, they frequently talk about their fears of people of color, the social incompetence they feel in racially mixed situations, the alienation they have experienced between parents and children when a child marries into a family of color, and the interracial friendships they had as children that were lost in adolescence or young adulthood without their ever understanding why. White people are paying a significant price for the system of advantage. The cost is not as high for Whites as it is for people of color, but a price is being paid. Wendell Berry, a White writer raised in Kentucky, captures this psychic pain in the opening pages of his book, *The Hidden Wound:*

> If white people have suffered less obviously from racism than black people, they have nevertheless suffered greatly; the cost has been greater perhaps than we can yet know. If the white man has inflicted the wound of racism upon black men, the cost has been that he would receive the mirror image of that wound into himself. As the master, or as a member of the dominant race, he has felt little compulsion to acknowledge it or speak of it; the more painful it has grown the more deeply he has hidden it within himself. But the wound is there, and it is a profound disorder, as great a damage in his mind as it is in his society.

The dismantling of racism is in the best interests of everyone.

A Word About Language

Throughout this chapter I have used the term *White* to refer to Americans of European descent. In another era, I might have used the term *Caucasian.* I have used the term *people of color* to refer to those groups in America that are and have been historically targeted by racism. This includes people of African descent, people of Asian descent, people of Latin American descent, and indigenous peoples (sometimes referred to as Native Americans or American Indians). Many people refer to these groups collectively as non-Whites. This term is particularly offensive because it defines groups of people in terms of what they are not. (Do we call women as "non-men?") I also avoid using the term *minorities* because it represents another kind of distortion of information which we need to correct. So-called minorities represent the majority of the world's population. While the term *people of color* is inclusive, it is not perfect. As a workshop participant once said, White people have color, too. Perhaps it would be more accurate to say "people of more color," though I am not ready to make that change. Perhaps fellow psychologist Linda James Myers is on the right track. She refers to two groups of people, those of acknowledged African descent and those of unacknowledged African descent, reminding us that we can all trace the roots of our common humanity to Africa.

I refer to people of acknowledged African descent as Black. I know that *African American* is also a commonly used term, and I often refer to myself and other Black people born and raised in America in that way. Perhaps because I am a child of the 1960s "Black and beautiful" era, I still prefer *Black.* The term is more inclusive than *African American,* because there are Black people in the United States who are not African American—Afro-Caribbeans, for example—yet are targeted by racism, and are identified as Black.

When referring to other groups of color, I try to use the terms that the people themselves want to be called. In some cases, there is no clear consensus. For example, some people of Latin American ancestry prefer *Latino,* while others prefer *Hispanic* or, if of Mexican descent, *Chicano.* The terms *Latino* and *Hispanic* are used interchangeably here. Similarly, there are regional variations in the use of the terms *Native American, American Indian,* and *Indian. American Indian* and *Native people* are now more widely used than *Native American,* and the language used here reflects that. People of Asian descent include Pacific Islanders, and that is reflected in the terms *Asian/Pacific Islanders* and *Asian Pacific Americans.* However, when quoting others I use whichever terms they use.

My dilemma about the language to use reflects the fact that race is a social construction. Despite myths to the contrary, biologists tell us that the only meaningful racial categorization is that of human. Van den Berghe defines race as "a group that is socially defined but on the basis of *physical* criteria," including skin color and facial features.

Racial identity development, a central focus of this book, usually refers to the process of defining for oneself the personal significance and social meaning of belonging to a particular racial group. The terms *racial identity* and *ethnic identity* are often used synonymously, though a distinction can be made between the two. An ethnic group is a socially defined group based on *cultural* criteria such as language, customs, and shared history. An individual might identify as a member of an ethnic group (Irish or Italian, for example) but might not think of himself in racial terms (as White). On the other hand, one may recognize the personal significance of racial group membership (identifying as Black, for instance) but may not consider ethnic identity (such as West Indian) as particularly meaningful.

Both racial and ethnic categories are socially constructed, and social definitions of these categories have changed over time. For example, in his book *Ethnic Identity: The Transformation of White America,* Richard Alba points out that the high rates of intermarriage and the dissolution of other social boundaries among European ethnic groups in the United States have reduced the significance of ethnic identity for these groups. In their place, he argues, a new ethnic identity is emerging, that of European American.

Throughout this book, I refer primarily to racial identity. It is important, however, to acknowledge that ethnic identity and racial identity sometimes intersect. For example, dark-skinned Puerto Ricans may identify culturally as Puerto Rican and yet be categorized racially by others as Black on the basis of physical appearance. In the case of either racial or ethnic identity, these identities remain most salient to individuals of racial or ethnic groups that have been historically disadvantaged or marginalized.

The language we use to categorize one another racially is imperfect. These categories are still evolving as the current debate over Census classifications indicates. The original creation of racial categories was in the service of oppression. Some may argue that to continue to use them is to continue that oppression. I respect that argument. Yet it is difficult to talk about what is essentially a flawed and problematic social construct without using language that is itself problematic. We have to be able to talk about it in order to change it. So this is the language I choose.

Questions for Discussion

1. After reading about the history and influence of "race" in the previous two chapters, how do you explain the perspectives of *Dr. Tatum's students* regarding race and racism? Did the students' reactions seem familiar?

2. What is "prejudice" according to Tatum? Is prejudice a major cause of racism and discrimination? If not, what is the relationship between "prejudice" and "race"?

3. In reference to all three readings, how does a history of categorizing people by "race" relate to "internalized oppression" described by Tatum?

4. According to Tatum, what are some aspects of the way that white people experience "race"? For example, what does "a system of advantage based on race" mean? What is the relationship of feeling "just normal" and having "an advantage"?

5. What are some aspects of the way people of color experience "race"? Does Tatum's idea of "walking against the current" on the moving walkway (being actively antiracist) apply to people of color as well?

6. In Tatum's "conversations about race" what were the most useful ideas for your everyday life? What were the most challenging?

PART II

Thinking Critically about Racism

Luke Tripp, Ph.D.

A Critical Framework of Racism in America

What is racism and what role does it play in shaping the American experience? Racism as both a concept and a condition will be discussed. It is a complex concept that includes several dimensions. The key ideas are race, political power, hierarchy, and control. Beginning with the notion of race, we can think of it as a biosocial construct that involves sorting individuals into hierarchal racial categories based on selected phenotypic characteristics that characterize different racial groups. These racial categories are arbitrarily defined and dubiously ranked by a dominant group on human attributes such as intelligence, morality, creativity, and compassion. The racial group assigned to in the highest category has the greatest amount of power and it uses power to control the other racial groups and to serve its own interests at the expense of the lower ranked racial groups. One axiom is that racism has very little to do with biology per se. It is the sociological meanings imputed to racial categories, which are based on arbitrary selected biological physical characteristics that are significant. In sum, racism involves evaluating, ranking, and ascribing behavior to individuals and groups on the basis of their presumed racial identity and rationalizing and justifying the dehumanization and exploitation of subordinate racial groups.

The Racial Classification Dilemma

Racial amalgamation is becoming more widespread, resulting in a racial identity crisis or racial identity confusion for a significant proportion of the population. It is becoming increasingly difficult for mixed race individuals to sort themselves into the official racial categories and for others to accurately identify the race of many individuals. These racial sorting and identification problems at the perceptual level demonstrate the social nature and the ambiguity of the construction of race. In addition, the political aspect of the construction of race is evident by the American government's own arbitrary racial classification system. The sociopolitical meanings of the different racial categories are changing as the demographics of America change. With a rapidly growing proportion of the population being comprised of people of color, who are playing an increasingly political role, we should expect that white privilege would be more difficult to maintain.

Forms of Racial Consciousness

The dialectics of American race consciousness: along the spectrum of American race consciousness are two polar opposite forms, racist and antiracist. The racist form represents the dominant racial ideology, which is based on the conventional racial stereotypes and embraces white supremacy. By contrast, the antiracist form of race consciousness is subversive. It abhors white supremacy and repudiates racial stereotypes.

Power of Racism

With this basic working notion of racism, we can approach the study of American racism.

The major forces that shape the daily lives of Americans are cultural, social, economic, and political. All of these forces have a prominent racial aspect, which shapes directly or indirectly the lives of virtually every individual and group in America. Race plays an important role in forming social patterns, families, religious groups, friendship circles, neighborhoods, educational institutions, workplaces, and government structures. To help us understand how and why these racial patterns and formations exists and persist, the three articles that follow provide descriptions, facts, and analyses that illustrate the power of racism in shaping the experiences of Americans.

Introduction: The Strange Enigma of Race in Contemporary America

How is it that racial inequality remains so pervasive and enormous when virtually all the public institutions, corporations, and white individuals claim not to be racist? Bonilla-Silva analyzes this contradiction by examining the beliefs and attitudes of white Americans. He describes how and why most whites justify or rationalize racial inequality in America.

Bonilla-Silva argues that during the period of government sanction racial segregation the social practices and mechanism of American society were justified and explained by an explicit white ideology of innate black inferiority. Now he asserts that the dominant racial ideology of whites in America can be characterized as a color blind ideology, which down plays or denies that race is a powerful determinate of the life chances of people of color. He claims that this ideology provides nonracial explanations, rationalizations, and justifications for racial disparities in the American socioeconomic stratification system.

CHAPTER 5

The Strange Enigma of Race in Contemporary America

Eduardo Bonilla-Silva

> There is a strange kind of enigma associated with the problem of racism. No one, or almost no one, wishes to see themselves as racist; still, racism persists, real and tenacious.
>
> —Albert Memmi, *Racism*

Racism without "Racists"

Nowadays, except for members of white supremacist organizations, few whites in the United States claim to be "racist." Most whites assert they "don't see any color, just people"; that although the ugly face of discrimination is still with us, it is no longer the central factor determining minorities' life chances; and, finally, that like Dr. Martin Luther King Jr., they aspire to live in a society where "people are judged by the content of their character, not by the color of their skin." More poignantly, most whites insist that minorities (especially blacks) are the ones responsible for whatever "race problem" we have in this country. They publicly denounce blacks for "playing the race card," for demanding the maintenance of unnecessary and divisive race-based programs, such as affirmative action, and for crying "racism" whenever they are criticized by whites. Most whites believe that if blacks and other minorities would just stop thinking about the past, work hard, and complain less (particularly about racial discrimination), then Americans of all hues could "all get along."

But regardless of whites' "sincere fictions," racial considerations shade almost everything in America. Blacks and dark-skinned racial minorities lag well behind whites in virtually every area of social life; they are about three times more likely to be poor than whites, earn about 40 percent less than whites, and have about a tenth of the net worth that whites have. They also receive an inferior education compared to whites, even when they attend integrated institutions. In terms of housing, black-owned units comparable to white-owned ones are valued at 35 percent less. Blacks and Latinos also have less access to the entire housing market because whites, through a variety of exclusionary practices by white realtors and homeowners, have been successful in effectively limiting their entrance into many neighborhoods. Blacks receive impolite treatment in stores, in restaurants, and in a host of other commercial transactions. Researchers have also documented that blacks pay more for goods such as cars and houses than do whites. Finally, blacks and dark-skinned Latinos are the targets of racial profiling by the police that, combined with the highly racialized criminal court system, guarantees their overrepresentation among those arrested, prosecuted, incarcerated, and if charged for a capital crime, executed. Racial profiling in the highways has become such a prevalent phenomenon that a term has emerged to describe it: driving while black. In short, blacks and most minorities are, "at the bottom of the well."

How is it possible to have this tremendous degree of racial inequality in a country where most whites claim that race is no longer relevant? More important, how do whites explain the apparent contradiction between their professed color blindness and the United States' color-coded inequality? In this book I attempt to answer both of these questions. I contend that whites have developed powerful explanations—which have ultimately become justifications—for contemporary racial inequality that exculpate them from any responsibility for the status of people of color. These explanations emanate from a new racial ideology that I label *colorblind racism*. This ideology, which acquired cohesiveness and dominance in the late 1960s, explains contemporary racial inequality as the outcome of nonracial dynamics. Whereas Jim Crow racism explained blacks' social standing as the result of their biological and moral inferiority, color-blind racism avoids such facile arguments. Instead, whites rationalize minorities' contemporary status as the product of market dynamics, naturally occurring phenomena, and blacks' imputed cultural limitations. For instance, whites can attribute Latinos' high poverty rate to a relaxed work ethic ("the Hispanics are mañana, mañana, mañana—tomorrow, tomorrow, tomorrow") or residential segregation as the result of natural tendencies among groups ("Does a cat and a dog mix? I can't see it. You can't drink milk and scotch. Certain mixes don't mix.").

Color-blind racism became the dominant racial ideology as the mechanisms and practices for keeping blacks and other racial minorities "at the bottom of the well" changed. I have argued elsewhere that contemporary racial inequality is reproduced through "new racism" practices that are subtle, institutional, and apparently nonracial. In contrast to the Jim Crow era, where racial inequality was enforced through overt means (e.g., signs saying "No Niggers Welcomed Here" or shotgun diplomacy at the voting booth), today racial practices operate in "now you see it, now you don't" fashion. For example, residential segregation, which is almost as high today as it was in the past, is no longer accomplished through overtly discriminatory practices. Instead, covert behaviors such as not showing all the available units, steering minorities and whites into certain neighborhoods, quoting higher rents or prices to minority applicants, or not advertising units at all are the weapons of choice to maintain separate communities. In the economic field, "smiling face" discrimination ("We don't have jobs now, but please check later"), advertising job openings in mostly white networks and ethnic newspapers, and steering highly educated people of color into poorly remunerated jobs or jobs with limited opportunities for mobility are the new ways of keeping minorities in a secondary position. Politically, although the Civil Rights struggles have helped remove many of the obstacles for the electoral participation of people of color, "racial gerrymandering, multimember legislative districts, election runoffs, annexation of predominantly white areas, at-large district elections, and anti–single-shot devices (disallowing concentrating votes in one or two candidates in cities using at-large elections) have become standard practices to disenfranchise" people of color. Whether in banks, restaurants, school admissions, or housing transactions, the maintenance of white privilege is done in a way that defies facile racial readings. Hence, the contours of color-blind racism fit America's "new racism" quite well.

Compared to Jim Crow racism, the ideology of color blindness seems like "racism lite." Instead of relying on name calling (niggers, Spics, Chinks), color-blind racism otherizes softly ("these people are human, too"); instead of proclaiming God placed minorities in the world in a servile position, it suggests they are behind because they do not work hard enough; instead of viewing interracial marriage as wrong on a straight racial basis, it regards it as "problematic" because of concerns over the children, location, or the extra burden it places on couples. Yet this new ideology has become a formidable political tool for the maintenance of the racial order. Much as Jim

Crow racism served as the glue for defending a brutal and overt system of racial oppression in the pre–Civil Rights era, color-blind racism serves today as the ideological armor for a covert and institutionalized system in the post–Civil Rights era. And the beauty of this new ideology is that it aids in the maintenance of white privilege without fanfare, without naming those who it subjects and those who it rewards. It allows a President to state things such as, "I strongly support diversity of all kinds, including racial diversity in higher education," yet, at the same time, to characterize the University of Michigan's affirmation action program as "flawed" and "discriminatory" against whites. Thus whites enunciate positions that safeguard their racial interests without sounding "racist." Shielded by color blindness, whites can express resentment toward minorities; criticize their morality, values, and work ethic; and even claim to be the victims of "reverse racism." This is the thesis I will defend in this book to explain the curious enigma of "racism without racists."

Whites' Racial Attitudes in the Post–Civil Rights Era

Since the late 1950s, surveys on racial attitudes have consistently found that fewer whites subscribe to the views associated with Jim Crow. For example, whereas the majority of whites supported segregated neighborhoods, schools, transportation, jobs, and public accommodations in the 1940s, less than a quarter indicated they did in the 1970s. Similarly, fewer whites than ever now seem to subscribe to stereotypical views of blacks. Although the number is still high (ranging from 20 percent to 50 percent, depending on the stereotype), the proportion of whites who state in surveys that blacks are lazy, stupid, irresponsible, and violent has declined since the 1940s.

These changes in whites' racial attitudes have been explained by the survey community and commentators in four ways. First, are the *racial optimists*. This group of analysts agrees with whites' common sense on racial matters and believes the changes symbolize a profound transition in the United States. Early representatives of this view were Herbert Hyman and Paul B. Sheatsley, who wrote widely influential articles on the subject in *Scientific American.* In a reprint of their earlier work in the influential collection edited by Talcott Parsons and Kenneth Clark, *The Negro American,* Sheatsely rated the changes in white attitudes as "revolutionary" and concluded,

> The mass of white Americans have shown in many ways that they will not follow a racist government and that they will not follow racist leaders. Rather, they are engaged in the painful task of adjusting to an integrated society. It will not be easy for most, but one cannot at this late date doubt the basic commitment. In their hearts they know that the American Negro is right.

In recent times, Glenn Firebaugh and Kenneth Davis, Seymour Lipset, and Paul Sniderman and his coauthors, in particular, have carried the torch for racial optimists. Firebaugh and Davis, for example, based on their analysis of survey results from 1972 to 1984, concluded that the trend toward less antiblack prejudice was across the board. Sniderman and his coauthors, as well as Lipset, go a step further than Firebaugh and Davis because they have openly advocated color-blind politics as *the* way to settle the United States' racial dilemmas. For instance, Sniderman and Edward Carmines made this explicit appeal in their recent book, *Reaching Beyond Race,*

> To say that a commitment to a color-blind politics is worth undertaking is to call for a politics centered on the needs of those most in need. It is not to argue for a politics in which race is irrelevant, but in favor of one in which race is relevant so far as it is a gauge of need. Above all, it is a call for a politics which, because it is organized around moral principles that apply regardless of race, can be brought to bear with special force on the issue of race.

The problems with this optimistic interpretation are twofold. First, as I have argued elsewhere, relying on questions that were framed in the Jim Crow era to assess whites' racial views today produces an artificial image of progress. Since the central racial debates and the language used to debate those matters have changed, our analytical focus ought to be dedicated to the analysis of the new racial issues. Insisting on the need to rely on old questions to keep longitudinal (trend) data as the basis for analysis will, by default, produce a rosy picture of race relations that misses what is going on the ground. Second, and more important, because of the change in the normative climate in the post–Civil Rights era, analysts must exert extreme caution when interpreting attitudinal data, particularly when it comes from single-method research designs. The research strategy that seems more appropriate for our times is mixed research designs (surveys used in combination with interviews, ethnosurveys, etc.), because it allows researchers to cross-examine their results.

A second, more numerous group of analysts exhibit what I have labeled elsewhere as the *racial pesoptimist* position. Racial pesoptimists attempt to strike a "balanced" view and suggest that whites' racial attitudes reflect progress and resistance. The classical example of this stance is Howard Schuman. Schuman has argued for more than thirty years that whites' racial attitudes involve a mixture of tolerance and intolerance, of acceptance of the principles of racial liberalism (equal opportunity for all, end of segregation, etc.) and a rejection of the policies that would make those principles a reality (from affirmative action to busing).

Despite the obvious appeal of this view in the research community (the appearance of neutrality, the pondering of "two sides," and this view's "balanced" component), racial pesoptimists are just closet optimists. Schuman, for example, has pointed out that, although "White responses to questions of principle are . . . more complex than is often portrayed . . . they nevertheless do show in almost every instance a positive movement over time." Furthermore, it is his belief that the normative change in the United States is real and that the issue is that whites are having a hard time translating those norms into personal preferences.

A third group of analysts argues that the changes in whites' attitudes represent the emergence of a *symbolic racism.* This tradition is associated with the work of David Sears and his associate, Donald Kinder. They have defined symbolic racism as "a blend of anti-black affect and the kind of traditional American moral values embodied in the Protestant Ethic." According to these authors, symbolic racism has replaced biological racism as the primary way whites express their racial resentment toward minorities. In Kinder and Sanders's words:

> A new form of prejudice has come to prominence, one that is preoccupied with matters of moral character, informed by the virtues associated with the traditions of individualism. At its center are the contentions that blacks do not try hard enough to overcome the difficulties they face and that they take what they have not earned. Today, we say, prejudice is expressed in the language of American individualism.

Authors in this tradition have been criticized for the slipperiness of the concept "symbolic racism," for claiming that the blend of antiblack affect and individualism is new, and for not explaining why symbolic racism came about. The first critique, developed by Howard Schuman, is that the concept has been "defined and operationalized in complex and varying ways." Despite this conceptual slipperiness, indexes of symbolic racism have been found to be in fact different from those of old-fashioned racism and to be strong predictors of whites' opposition to affirmative action. The two other critiques, made forcefully by Lawrence Bobo, have been partially addressed by Kinder and Sanders in their recent book, *Divided by Color.* First, Kinder and Sanders, as well as

Sears, have made clear that their contention is not that this is the first time in history that antiblack affect and elements of the American Creed have combined. Instead, their claim is that this combination has become *central* to the new face of racism. Regarding the third critique, Kinder and Sanders go at length to explain the transition from old-fashioned to symbolic racism. Nevertheless, their explanation hinges on arguing that changes in blacks' tactics (from civil disobedience to urban violence) led to an onslaught of a new form of racial resentment that later found more fuel in controversies over welfare, crime, drugs, family, and affirmative action. What is missing in this explanation is a materially based explanation for why these changes occurred. Instead, their theory of prejudice is rooted in the "process of socialization and the operation of routine cognitive and emotional psychological processes."

Yet, despite its limitations, the symbolic racism tradition has brought attention to key elements of how whites explain racial inequality today. Whether this is "symbolic" of antiblack affect or not is beside the point and hard to assess, since as a former student of mine queried, "How does one test for the unconscious?"

The fourth explanation of whites' contemporary racial attitudes is associated with those who claim that whites' racial views represent a *sense of group position.* This position, forcefully advocated by Lawrence Bobo and James Kluegel, is similar to Jim Sidanius's "social dominance" and Mary Jackman's "group interests" arguments. In essence, the claim of all these authors is that white prejudice is an ideology to defend white privilege. Bobo and his associates have specifically suggested that because of socioeconomic changes that transpired in the 1950s and 1960s, a *laissez-faire racism* emerged that was fitting of the United States' "modern, nationwide, postindustrial free labor economy and polity." Laissez-faire racism "encompasses an ideology that blames blacks themselves for their poorer relative economic standing, seeing it as the function of perceived cultural inferiority."

Some of the basic arguments of authors in the symbolic and modern racism traditions and, particularly, of the laissez-faire racism view are fully compatible with my color-blind racism interpretation. As these authors, I argue that color-blind racism has rearticulated elements of traditional liberalism (work ethic, rewards by merit, equal opportunity, individualism, etc.) for racially illiberal goals. I also argue like them that whites today rely more on cultural rather than biological tropes to explain blacks' position in this country. Finally, I concur with most analysts of post–Civil Rights' matters in arguing that whites do not perceive discrimination to be a central factor shaping blacks' life chances.

Although most of my differences with authors in the symbolic racism and laissez-faire traditions are methodological (see below), I have one central theoretical disagreement with them. Theoretically, most of these authors are still snarled in the prejudice problematic and thus interpret actors' racial views as *individual psychological* dispositions. Although Bobo and his associates have a conceptualization that is closer to mine, they still retain the notion of prejudice and its psychological baggage rooted in interracial hostility. In contrast, my model is not anchored in actors' affective dispositions (although affective dispositions may be manifest or latent in the way many express their racial views). Instead, it is based on a materialist interpretation of racial matters and thus sees the views of actors as corresponding to their systemic location. Those at the bottom of the racial barrel tend to hold oppositional views and those who receive the manifold wages of whiteness tend to hold views in support of the racial status quo. Whether actors express "resentment" or "hostility" toward minorities is largely irrelevant for the maintenance of white privilege. As David Wellman points out in his *Portraits of White Racism,* "[p]rejudiced people are not the only racists in America."

Key Terms: Race, Racial Structure, and Racial Ideology

One reason why, in general terms, whites and people of color cannot agree on racial matters is because they conceive terms such as "racism" very differently. Whereas for most whites racism is prejudice, for most people of color racism is systemic or institutionalized. Although this is not a theory book, my examination of color-blind racism has etched in it the indelible ink of a "regime of truth" about how the world is organized. Thus, rather than hiding my theoretical assumptions, I state them openly for the benefit of readers and potential critics.

The first key term is the notion of *race*. There is very little formal disagreement among social scientists in accepting the idea that race is a socially constructed category. This means that notions of racial difference are human creations rather than eternal, essential categories. As such, racial categories have a history and are subject to change. And here ends the agreement among social scientists on this matter. There are at least three distinct variations on how social scientists approach this constructionist perspective on race. The first approach, which is gaining popularity among white social scientists, is the idea that because race is socially constructed, it is not a fundamental category of analysis and praxis. Some analysts go as far as to suggest that because race is a constructed category, then it is not real and social scientists who use the category are the ones who make it real.

The second approach, typical of most sociological writing on race, gives lip service to the social constructionist view—usually a line in the beginning of the article or book. Writers in this group then proceed to discuss "racial" differences in academic achievement, crime, and SAT scores as if they were truly racial. This is the central way in which contemporary scholars contribute to the propagation of racist interpretations of racial inequality. By failing to highlight the social dynamics that produce these racial differences, these scholars help reinforce the racial order.

The third approach, and the one I use in this book, acknowledges that race, as other social categories such as class and gender, is constructed but insists that it has a *social* reality. This means that after race—or class or gender—is created, it produces real effects on the actors racialized as "black" or "white." Although race, as other social constructions, is unstable, it has a "changing same" quality at its core.

In order to explain how a socially constructed category produces real race effects, I need to introduce a second key term: the notion of *racial structure.* When race emerged in human history, it formed a social structure (a racialized social system) that awarded systemic privileges to Europeans (the peoples who became "white") over non-Europeans (the peoples who became "nonwhite"). Racialized social systems, or white supremacy for short, became global and affected all societies where Europeans extended their reach. I therefore conceive a society's racial structure as *the totality of the social relations and practices that reinforce white privilege.* Accordingly, the task of analysts interested in studying racial structures is to uncover the particular social, economic, political, social control, and ideological mechanisms responsible for the reproduction of racial privilege in a society.

But why are racial structures reproduced in the first place? Would not humans, after discovering the folly of racial thinking, work to abolish race as a category as well as a practice? Racial structures remain in place for the same reasons that other structures do. Since actors racialized as "white"—or as members of the dominant race—receive material benefits from the racial order, they struggle (or passively receive the manifold wages of whiteness) to maintain their privileges. In contrast, those defined as belonging to the subordinate race or races struggle to change the status quo (or become resigned to their position). Therein lies the secret of racial structures and racial inequality the world over. They exist because they benefit members of the dominant race.

If the ultimate goal of the dominant race is to defend its collective interests (i.e., the perpetuation of systemic white privilege), it should surprise no one that this group develops rationalizations to account for the status of the various races. And here I introduce my third key term, the notion of *racial ideology.* By this I mean *the racially based frameworks used by actors to explain and justify* (dominant race) or *challenge* (subordinate race or races) *the racial status quo.* Although all the races in a racialized social system have the *capacity* of developing these frameworks, the frameworks of the dominant race tend to become the master frameworks upon which *all* racial actors ground (for or against) their ideological positions. Why? Because as Marx pointed out in *The German Ideology,* "the ruling *material* force of society, is at the same time its ruling *intellectual* force." This does not mean that ideology is almighty. In fact, as I will show in chapter 6, ideological rule is always partial. Even in periods of hegemonic rule, such as the current one, subordinate racial groups develop oppositional views. However, it would be foolish to believe that those who rule a society do not have the power to at least color (pun intended) the views of the ruled.

Racial ideology can be conceived for analytical purposes as comprising the following elements: common frames, style, and racial stories (details on each can be found in chapters 2, 3, and 4). The frames that bond together a particular racial ideology are rooted in the group-based conditions and experiences of the races and are, at the symbolic level, the representations developed by these groups to explain how the world is or ought to be. And because the group life of the various racially defined groups is based on hierarchy and domination, the ruling ideology expresses as "common sense" the interests of the dominant race, while oppositional ideologies attempt to challenge that common sense by providing alternative frames, ideas, and stories based on the experiences of subordinated races.

Individual actors employ these elements as "building blocks . . . for manufacturing versions on actions, self, and social structures" in communicative situations. The looseness of the elements allows users to maneuver within various contexts (e.g., responding to a race-related survey, discussing racial issues with family, or arguing about affirmative action in a college classroom) and produce various accounts and presentations of self (e.g., appearing ambivalent, tolerant, or strong minded). This loose character enhances the legitimating role of racial ideology because it allows for accommodation of contradictions, exceptions, and new information. As Jackman points out about ideology in general: "Indeed, the strength of an ideology lies in its loose-jointed, flexible application. *An ideology is a political instrument, not an exercise in personal logic:* consistency is rigidity, the only pragmatic effect of which is to box oneself in."

Before I can proceed, two important caveats should be offered. First, although whites, because of their privileged position in the racial order, form a social group (the dominant race), they are fractured along class, gender, sexual orientation, and other forms of "social cleavage." Hence, they have multiple and often contradictory interests that are not easy to disentangle and that predict *a priori* their mobilizing capacity (Do white workers have more in common with white capitalists than with black workers?). However, because all actors awarded the dominant racial position, regardless of their multiple structural locations (men or women, gay or straight, working class or bourgeois) benefit from what Mills calls the "racial contract," *most* have historically endorsed the ideas that justify the racial status quo.

Second, although not every single member of the dominant race defends the racial status quo or spouts color-blind racism, *most* do. To explain this point by analogy, although not every capitalist defends capitalism (e.g., Frederick Engels, the coauthor of *The Communist Manifesto,* was a capitalist) and not every man defends patriarchy (e.g., *Achilles Heel* is an English magazine published by feminist men), *most* do in some fashion. In the same vein, although some whites fight white supremacy and do not endorse white common sense, *most* subscribe to substantial portions of it in a casual, uncritical fashion that helps sustain the prevailing racial order.

How to Study Color-Blind Racism

I will rely mostly on interview data to make my case. This choice is based on important conceptual and methodological considerations. Conceptually, my focus is examining whites' racial ideology, and ideology, racial or not, is produced and reproduced in communicative interaction. Hence, although surveys are useful instruments for gathering general information on actors' views, they are severely limited tools for examining how people explain, justify, rationalize, and articulate racial viewpoints. People are less likely to express their positions and emotions about racial issues by answering "yes" and "no" or "strongly agree" and "strongly disagree" to questions. Despite the gallant effort of some survey researchers to produce methodologically correct questionnaires, survey questions still restrict the free flow of ideas and unnecessarily constrain the range of possible answers for respondents.

Methodologically, I argue that because the normative climate in the post–Civil Rights era has made illegitimate the public expression of racially based feelings and viewpoints, surveys on racial attitudes have become like multiple-choice exams in which respondents work hard to choose the "right" answers (i.e., those that fit public norms). For instance, although a variety of data suggest racial considerations are central to whites' residential choices, more than 90 percent of whites state in surveys that they have no problem with the idea of blacks moving into their neighborhoods. Similarly, even though about 80 percent of whites claim they would not have a problem if a member of their family brought a black person home for dinner, research shows that (1) very few whites (fewer than 10 percent) can legitimately claim the proverbial "some of my best friends are blacks" and (2) whites rarely fraternize with blacks.

Of more import yet is insistence by mainstream survey researchers' on using questions developed in the 1950s and 1960s to assess changes in racial tolerance. This strategy is predicated on the assumption that "racism" (what I label here racial ideology) does not change over time. If instead one regards racial ideology as in fact changing, the reliance on questions developed to tackle issues from the Jim Crow era will produce an artificial image of progress and miss most of whites' contemporary racial nightmares.

Despite my conceptual and methodological concerns with survey research, I believe well-designed surveys are still useful instruments to glance at America's racial reality. Therefore, I report survey result from my own research projects as well as from research conducted by other scholars whenever appropriate. My point, then, is not to deny attitudinal change or to condemn to oblivion survey research on racial attitudes, but to understand whites' new racial beliefs and their implications as well as possible.

Questions for Discussion

1. What is the most important information in this article?

2. What are the key concepts we need to understand in this article?

3. What are the main assumptions underlying the author's thinking?

4. Evaluate the author's argument.

Blacks in America: American Mythology and Miseducation

Luke Tripp, Ph.D.

Introduction

Historical Roots of White Supremacy

In general, whites believe that European-based culture is superior. Their belief is based on the material evidence that their scientific knowledge and technology are the most advanced, which they have used to establish white supremacy through conquest, colonization, and domination of people of color around the world. They tend to make an illogical link between their technological superiority and their claims of genetic and moral superiority. These false claims serve as the basis of their feelings of racial superiority and their belief that they have an inherent right to rule the world on their "superior" moral value system.

Foundations of American Racism: America's Racial Birth Defects

A wealthy white male elite founded the United States of America on the principle of white supremacy. It established a governmental structure and a legal framework that was designed to maintain rule by a white male property owning class. In the formation of the United States of America two major racial policies were legalized. The first was a racial policy to relocate and confine Indians who had been subdued to impoverished reservations and exterminate those who resisted white control of their lands. The second policy was to control blacks and use their labor to build America for the benefit of white society, while stereotyping them as a menace to society. In the twenty-first century, the white elite continue to wield overwhelming political power in America. Their political dominance is based mainly on their economic power and the dominant ideology of inequality held by the majority of Americans.

Key Concepts

- Racism is embedded in American culture and the capitalist system. It is a core feature of American society.
- The underlying principle of American social organization is racial inequality.
- Racism is maintained consciously and unconsciously by social structures and stereotypes.
- Racism functions to solidify racial groups against each other.

- Government policies and structures and the mass media are the most powerful forces that shape race relations.
- Race refers to a group of people that is not universally defined in the same way. In the American historical experience, race refers to a group of people identified by a set of arbitrary selected physical characteristics that are common to a particular ancestral group.

American Racial Myths

American students are routinely and deliberately taught racial myths about American history. These myths play a very powerful role in perpetuating racism in American society. This article examines some major racist myths and their effects on race relations in America.

Unfortunately, most Americans have been woefully miseducated about their country. Much of what they believe about America is based on myths, lies, and slick propaganda. The process of miseducation begins very early in their lives and continues throughout their lifetimes. They are conditioned early in their preschool years to accept a fictional image of America through fairy tales, which portray imaginary heroes (white righteous knights) and villains (dark evil characters).

When children begin their formal education, they are routinely introduced to school rituals, which are designed to instill a sense of pride in America. Rarely are they introduced to ideas, which would stir intellectual curiosity about America. The fictional image of America that is presented to the young students is one that is lovable, but it is also one that is largely based on myths and deliberate lies. For instance, in many schools, students are required to stand with their hands across their hearts, while facing the American flag, and recite the pledge of allegiance to America. Included in this pledge are these words. ". . . one nation, under God, with liberty and justice for all." Every thinking person knows that this is patriotic rhetoric.

However, through repetition this big lie assumes the status of a quasi truth along with the fables about George Washington, the Father of America who "never told a lie." This all serves a major goal of American education, which is to teach students to love their country, but not to deeply understand it. It is no wonder that so many say "love it or leave it" to people who criticize America.

America: Community or Corporation

For most Americans, the origins of the country began when a group of "daring and righteous" English Pilgrims landed in 1620 at what is now called Plymouth, Massachusetts. Yet, the historical record shows that the first permanent English settlement was Jamestown, founded in the colony of Virginia in 1607. Why is this significant? This is significant because it serves to illustrate how the history of America is told in such a way as to make the story heroic. The story of a country founded by devoutly religious Christians dedicated to building a good society has greater patriotic appeal than the true story of a country whose origins are traced back to a settlement comprised of employees of the London Company and indentured servants whose task was to produce a profit for a group of English merchants. These merchants held an exclusive charter from King James I, which permitted them to exploit the resources of the land they seized from the Indians. In short, America began as a business venture motivated by greed and profit, not as an attempt to build a virtuous society based on community values (McLemore 1983, 22–5).

The First Charter of Virginia; April 10, 1606 (excerpt)

JAMES, by the Grace of God, King of England, Scotland, France and Ireland, Defender of the Faith, &c. WHEREAS our loving and well-disposed Subjects, Sir Thorn as Gales, and Sir George Somers, Knights, Richard Hackluit, Clerk, Prebendary of Westminster, and Edward-Maria Wingfield, Thomas Hanharm and Ralegh Gilbert, Esqrs. William Parker, and George Popham, Gentlemen, and divers others of our loving Subjects, have been humble Suitors unto us, that We would vouchsafe unto them our Licence, to make Habitation, Plantation, and to deduce a colony of sundry of our People into that part of America commonly called VIRGINIA, and other parts and Territories in America, either appertaining unto us, or which are not now actually possessed by any Christian Prince or People . . .

We, greatly commending, and graciously accepting of, their Desires for the Furtherance of so noble a Work, which may, by the Providence of Almighty God, hereafter tend to the Glory of his Divine Majesty, in propagating of Christian Religion to such People, as yet live in Darkness and miserable Ignorance of the true Knowledge and Worship of God, and may in time bring the Infidels and Savages, living in those parts, to human Civility, and to a settled and quiet Government: DO, by these our Letters Patents, graciously accept of, and agree to, their humble and well-intended Desires; . . .

And that they shall have all the Lands, Woods, Soil, Grounds, Havens, Ports, Rivers, Mines, Minerals, Marshes, Waters, Fishings, Commodities, and Hereditaments, whatsoever, from the said first Seat of their Plantation and Habitation by the Space of fifty Miles of English Statute Measure, all along the said Coast of Virginia and America, towards the West and Southwest, as the Coast lyeth, with all the Islands within one hundred Miles directly over against the same Sea Coast; And also all the Lands, Soil, Grounds, Havens, Ports, Rivers, Mines, Minerals, Woods, Waters, Marshes, Fishings, Commoditites, and Hereditaments, whatsoever, from the said Place of their first Plantation and Habitation for the space of fifty like English Miles, all alongst the said Coasts of Virginia and America, towards the East and Northeast, or towards the North, as the Coast lyeth, together with all the Islands within one hundred Miles, directly over against the said Sea Coast, And also all the Lands, Woods, Soil, Grounds, Havens, Ports, Rivers, Mines, Minerals, Marshes, Waters, Fishings, Commodities, and Hereditaments, whatsoever, from the same fifty Miles every way on the Sea Coast, directly into the main Land by the Space of one hundred like English Miles; And shall and may inhabit and remain there . . .

And moreover, we do GRANT and agree . . . that that the said several Councils of and for the said several Colonies, shall and lawfully may . . . give and take Order, to dig, mine, and search for all Manner of Mines of Gold, Silver, and Copper, as well within any Part of their said several Colonies . . .

Source: The Federal and State Constitutions Colonial Charters, and Other Organic Laws of the States, Territories, and Colonies Now or Heretofore Forming the United States of America Compiled and Edited Under the Act of Congress of June 30, 1906 by Francis Newton Thorpe Washington, DC : Government Printing Office, 1909.

http://avalon.law.yale.edu/17th_century/va01.asp [Accessed 10/30/2011]

Questions for Discussion

1. The territory granted by this charter is huge, but not unlimited. Why does King James exclude from his grant any lands "actually possessed by any Christian Prince or People"?
2. What does the charter imply about the people who already live on the lands being granted?
3. What is the primary purpose of the colony to be created by this charter?

Blacks and America's Origins

By omitting the story of Jamestown, the system of education ignores the beginning of the relationship between black people and white people in North America. Lerone Bennett, a black historian, has written a book entitled, *Before the Mayflower*, to make a historical point that black people were brought in shackles to Jamestown in 1619 before the Pilgrims landed at Plymouth in 1620. But, unlike the Pilgrims who, in their quest for freedom, were in the process of shaping their own future. Black people were taken forcibly in chains to Jamestown to work for those who owned them. Theirs was a future with little, if any, freedom (Bennett 1984).

The main historical point, however, is that relations between blacks and whites in America began as a relationship based on whites debasement of and control over black people and that this basic relationship has persisted to the present. This profound and obvious fact cannot be ignored if we are to fully understand the political, psychological, social, and economic dynamics of U.S. society.

Once this is acknowledged, it becomes easier to understand the nature of the cultural dynamics of America and the rhetoric of the American ruling elite. The ruling elite continues to promote an image of America as a country firmly committed to the humanitarian values of freedom, justice, liberty, and democracy. But, the reality is that America is a ruthlessly competitive society driven by the pursuit of material wealth, social status, power, and control. Further, it is a hierarchical society destructively divided along racial and class lines. This was the reality in Jamestown in the early 1600s when America was in its embryonic stage, and it is more of a reality today.

George Washington and King George III

The sanitized image of America is built with a chronological sequence of myths and distortions. As the story continues, the American Revolution is falsely presented as a righteous struggle of American colonists against British tyranny. George Washington is portrayed as a hero who fought to end oppression under the rule of King George III. This struggle was actually a power struggle between dominant elites who shared more social class similarities than differences. Let us think of King George III and George Washington as representing two belligerent forces and compare them in terms of their social positions, values, and interests. King George III was a monarch who ruled over a growing empire. He was seeking greater power, control, and wealth. He was not concerned about sharing power or wealth with the masses of his subjects.

When we examine the life of George Washington, we see he had much in common with his adversary, King George III. George Washington was born into a wealthy family and pursued greater wealth and more power throughout his life. His subjects, who were under his absolute control, were hundreds of black slaves who lived wretched lives in a state of total degradation on his tobacco plantation in Virginia. He was one of the biggest, if not the biggest, slave owner in America during his time (Fresia, 1988).

From this we see that both Georges shared similar values and interests. However, their primary interests had little to do with lofty values and beliefs in freedom, justice, liberty, and the dignity of humankind. Moreover, a critical examination of the American Revolution reveals a struggle for more political power, economic control, and material wealth between two elite groups rather than a heroic struggle between the forces of freedom and tyranny. The only people who fought for basic humanitarian values in that war were blacks.

Origins of "Free" Black People

Throughout the period of slavery there was a small class of blacks who were not slaves. This class resulted from the bold moves of some slaves who liberated themselves by running away and from the actions of some slave masters who either freed their slaves or allowed their slaves to earn money to purchase their own freedom. In addition, through natural reproduction this class of blacks perpetuated itself.

Blacks and the American Revolution

The role of blacks in the American Revolution is interesting. During the early stages of the Revolutionary War, George Washington and the colonists had a policy of excluding "free" black men from their army. But their foe, the British, adopted the opposite policy of recruiting "free" blacks to fight in the King's army and promising runaway slaves freedom if they served. Realizing that their policy of black exclusion put them at a serious disadvantage, Washington and the colonists reversed their policy and adopted a policy similar to that of the British. Many black historians proudly state that over 5,000 blacks fought in Washington's army, but few mention that over 20,000 served in the British army. The main point, however, is rarely made; the only people fighting for basic human rights on either side were black. It should also be remembered that contrary to the simplistic picture found in textbooks and Hollywood movies, the white colonists were also divided over the war and many fought with the British.

Declaration of Independence, July 4, 1776

Americans are almost all familiar with this portion of the Declaration, penned by Thomas Jefferson in 1776:

We Hold These Truths to be Self-Evident:

That all men are created equal; that they are endowed by their Creator with certain unalienable rights; that among these are life, liberty, and the pursuit of happiness; that, to secure these rights, governments are instituted among men, deriving their just powers from the consent of the governed; that whenever any form of government becomes destructive of these ends, it is the right of the people to alter or to abolish it, and to institute new government, laying its foundation on such principles, and organizing its powers in such form, as to them shall seem most likely to effect their safety and happiness.

We may be less familiar, however with the long list of charges against King George III that follow. Most of the charges relate to political abuses, for example:

He has refused his assent to laws, the most wholesome and necessary for the public good.
He has forbidden his governors to pass laws of immediate and pressing importance, unless suspended in their operation till his assent should be obtained; and, when so suspended, he has utterly neglected to attend to them. . . .

(continued)

He has erected a multitude of new offices, and sent hither swarms of officers to harass our people and eat out their substance.

The final charge, however, is not about governance:

He has excited domestic insurrection among us, and has endeavored to bring on the inhabitants of our frontiers the merciless Indian savages, whose known rule of warfare is an undistinguished destruction of all ages, sexes, and conditions.

Declaration text from http://avalon.law.yale.edu/18th_century/declare.asp [accessed 10/30/11]

Questions for Discussion

1. Compare the opening lines of this excerpt from the final lines. What do you think Jefferson believed about human equality?
2. "Domestic insurrections" is not a phrase we use commonly in the 21st century. It means a rebellion at home. What kind of rebellion at home would be most frightening to a plantation owner like Jefferson?
3. Who are the "us" and "we" in the Declaration?
4. Were you taught about the last paragraph above in your high-school history or government classes? Who made the decision about what you would be taught?

Blacks and the American Constitution

There is probably no greater myth in American history than the one about the American Constitution. Americans glorify this historical document as a model of democratic principles that should be emulated by all countries seeking to become democratic. Moreover, it is praised as a guarantor of human rights and a protector against tyranny and oppression. The Framers of the American Constitution are likewise revered as compassionate, democratically minded, fatherly figures, who were primarily interested in the well-being of others. These very powerful images work very well among the miseducated. The American education establishment as well as the mass media systematically foster these images to perpetuate the illusion that America is a democratic country founded by honorable men.

Even a cursory look at black history provides insights, which quickly debunk the myths about the American Constitution and the "Founding Fathers." There are three sections in the American Constitution that legitimize the dehumanization of black people. First, Article I, Section 2 stipulates that black slaves (the Framers carefully avoided using the term slave in the constitution) would be counted as three-fifths of a person for the purpose of distributing power among the white ruling elite; second, Article I, Section 9 provided for the protection of the slave trade; and third, Article IV, Section 2 declared runaway slaves (freedom seekers, refugees) to be criminals who had to be returned to their slave master. Thus, the legal foundation for racism was firmly set in the American Constitution. But, this would come as no surprise if one studied historical facts rather than fiction.

Race, Slavery, and the Constitution

The words "slave" and "slavery" are absent from the U.S. Constitution. Nevertheless, there are three clear references to slavery. Can you find the slaves in the passage below?

Art. 1: sec. 2: "Representatives and direct taxes shall be apportioned among the several States which may be included within this Union, according to their respective numbers, which shall be determined by adding to the whole number of free persons, including those bound to service for a term of years, and excluding Indians not taxed, three fifths of all other persons."

Art. 1, sec. 9: "The migration or importation of such persons as any of the States now existing shall think proper to admit, shall not be prohibited by the Congress prior to the year one thousand eight hundred and eight; but a tax or duty may be imposed on such importation, not exceeding ten dollars for each person."

Art 4, sec. 2: "No person held to service or labor in one State, under the laws thereof, escaping into another, shall, in consequence of any law or regulation therein, be discharged from such service or labor, but shall be delivered up, on claim of the party to whom such service or labor may be due."

Questions for Discussion

1. Article I, sec. 2 counts each slave as 3/5 of a person for purposes of allocating seats in the House of Representatives. Does that mean the slaves got 3/5 of the political rights of free people? Which states got extra representation from this clause?
2. Article I, sec. 9 protected the trans-Atlantic slave trade from federal interference until 1808, at which point the federal government promptly banned it. Did ending the slave trade end slavery in the United States?
3. The old Articles of Confederation did not let the national government force the states to do anything. In Article 4, sec. 2, the new Constitution requires the free states to do something they did not have to do before. What did the free states have to do?
4. On balance, was the Constitution as originally written proslavery, antislavery, or neutral?

The Elite and the American Constitution

Who were the Framers of the Constitution? This is a concrete question. Were there any women among them? No. Were there any people of color among them? No. Were there any poor white men (those who did not own property) among them? No. The historical record will show that the "Founding Fathers" were a group of powerful, privileged wealthy white men, some of whom were slave masters, including George Washington and Thomas Jefferson. This helps explain why the Constitution was a proslavery, antidemocratic document primarily designed to sanction and protect the interests of the wealthy white ruling elite.

Blacks and the American Justice System

Students are taught that the American system of justice is the fairest in the world, one worthy of emulation. This image enjoys credibility despite the fact that historically the courts sanctioned the most dehumanizing form of slavery until the end of the Civil War in 1865. And then after slavery, the courts legalized a demeaning form of racial segregation.

The American legal establishment has always been antiblack. It has never respected black people as first-class American citizens. For about 250 years, American laws legalized the enslavement and debasement of black people. During this long period of slavery, the courts defined black people as subhuman (Barker and McCorry 1980, 14). The legal opinion that best articulates this view is documented in the written decision of the U.S. Supreme Court in the Dred Scott case (*Dred Scott v. Sandford* (60 U.S. 393. 19 How. 393, 1857). In this case, the Supreme Court declared that the American Constitution does not recognize black people as human beings worthy of the rights and privileges of citizenship.

The Court Stated That:

> They had for more than a century before been regarded as being of an inferior order; and altogether unfit to associate with the white race, either in social or political relations; and so far inferior that they had no rights which the white man was bound to respect; and that the negro might justly and lawfully be reduced to slavery for his benefit. He was bought and sold, and treated as an ordinary article of merchandise and traffic, whenever a profit could be made by it. This opinion was at that time fixed and universal in the civilized portion of the white race. It was regarded as an axiom in morals as well as in politics, which no one thought of disputing, or supposed to be open to dispute; and men in every grade and position in society daily and habitually acted upon it in their private pursuits, as well as in matters of public concern, without doubting for a moment the correctness of this opinion . . .

Is there any wonder that black people have always had and continue to have serious problems with the criminal justice system? From the point of contact with the police to the harsh sentence of the judge, black people regularly experience both prosecution and persecution.

Illusions about the Civil War

There are two widespread beliefs about the Civil War; the War was fought to free the slaves, and President Abraham Lincoln freed the slaves. These beliefs suggest the following:

- The white community in the North was willing to sacrifice thousands of white lives to free black people from slavery.
- The United States government was willing to risk its internal cohesion as a nation to free black people from slavery.
- White Northerners were willing to suffer severe economic deprivation for the sake of the welfare of black people.
- White Northerners had deep compassion for blacks.
- Freeing the slaves was a political goal of Lincoln's, moreover, the major one.

- He was willing to risk his presidency and the future of the federal government to free the slaves.
- He operated on his best moral impulses.

These characterizations conjure up an image of a government and people who had great moral fortitude. They are the stuff necessary for a good heroic story. Let us examine the historical facts.

It is ironic that perhaps the biggest American myths have to do with black freedom. From grade school, students are taught to believe that the bloodiest war in American history, the Civil War, was fought for the honorable goal of freeing black people from slavery. This fiction is embellished with the fabrication that President Abraham Lincoln freed black people. The truth is that the abolition of slavery was a consequence of the Civil War, not a primary cause, and Lincoln did not actually free one slave. These myths persist and largely go unchallenged because they have been so cleverly woven into the American cultural matrix of political ideology and moral values. Furthermore, they have retained credibility because they were created with deceptive half-truths and distortions.

The historical record reveals that the central causes of the Civil War were related to conflicting political and economic interests between the white ruling elite in the Southern states and the white ruling elite in the Northern states. These two elites struggled over the distribution of political power in an ever-expanding country and the role of federal authority at the state and territorial levels. This conflict became so intense that it ruptured the country and resulted in the Civil War (Franklin and Moss 1988, 176–80).

Blacks and Abraham Lincoln

Although Abraham Lincoln had a long history of opposition to slavery, he was not at the cutting edge of the movement to abolish slavery. Lincoln, who believed that slavery was a cruel institution, which undermined the moral integrity of the white nation, can be classified as a moderate in the abolitionist movement against slavery. He thought that it might be possible to abolish slavery by using a slow gradual approach coupled with compensating slave owners for their slaves and by relocating black people outside the United States (Franklin 1980, 212–14).

His approach was criticized by the militant abolitionists, who wanted the immediate nullification of slave laws and the use of force if necessary to bring slavery to a quick end. Further, they pressed for compensation to the slaves for their unpaid labor rather than to the undeserving slave owners, and they pushed for the legal recognition of black people as American citizens.

When Lincoln took office as President on March 4, 1861, the nation was breaking up. Seven states in the lower South had seceded and other slave states were moving in that direction. He perceived his principle task as bringing the seceded states back into the Union. To accomplish this, he prodded Congress to adopt an amendment to the Constitution that would have permanently barred Congress from ending slavery in the states (Geschwender 1978, 154).

Even after the Civil war began, Lincoln continued his conciliatory policy toward the Confederacy. When blacks volunteered their services to the Union army, they were rejected. Lincoln believed that allowing blacks to serve in the Union army would further alienate the Confederacy (Franklin and Moss 1988, 182). As the war became protracted, however, military and economic considerations compelled Lincoln to reverse his black exclusion policy.

Excerpts of Lincoln's Thoughts on Race and Slavery

First Lincoln-Douglas Debate
August 21, 1858
Ottawa, Illinois

. . . I will say here, while upon this subject, that I have no purpose directly or indirectly to interfere with the institution of slavery in the States where it exists. I believe I have no lawful right to do so, and I have no inclination to do so. I have no purpose to introduce political and social equality between the white and the black races. There is a physical difference between the two, which my judgment will probably forever forbid their living together upon the footing of perfect equality and inasmuch as it becomes necessary that there must be a difference, I, as well as Judge Douglas, am in favor of the race to which I belong, having the superior position. I have never said anything to the contrary, but I hold that notwithstanding all this, there is no reason in the world why the negro is not entitled to all the natural rights enumerated in the Declaration of Independence, the right to life, liberty and the pursuit of happiness. [Loud cheers.] I hold that he is as much entitled to these as the white man. I agree with Judge Douglas he is not my equal in many respects - certainly not in color, perhaps not in moral or intellectual endowment. But in the right to eat the bread, without leave of anybody else, which his own hand earns, *he is my equal and the equal of Judge Douglas and the equal of every living man.* [Great applause.] . . .

Fourth Lincoln-Douglas Debate
September 18, 1858

Charleston, Illinois

. . . I will say then that I am not, nor ever have been in favor or bringing about in any way the social and political equality of the white and black races, [applause]- that I am not nor ever have been in favor of making voters of jurors of negroes, nor of qualifying them to hold office, nor to intermarry with white people; and I will say in addition to this that there is a physical difference between white and black races which I believe will for ever forbid the two races living together on terms of social and political equality. And inasmuch as they cannot so live, while they do remain together there must be the position of superior and inferior, and I as much as any other man am in favor of having the superior position assigned to the white race. I say upon this occasion I do not perceive that because the white man is to have the superior position to the negro should be denied everything. I do not understand that because I do not want a negro woman for a slave I must necessarily want her for a wife. [Cheers and laughter.] My understanding is that I can just let her alone. I am now in my fiftieth year, and I certainly never have had a black woman for either a slave or a wife. So it seems to me quite possible for us to get along without making either slaver or wives of negroes. I will add to this that I have never seen to my knowledge a man, woman or child who was in favor of producing a perfect equality, social and political, between negroes and white men . . . I have never had the least apprehension that I or my friends would marry negroes if there was no law to keep them from it, [roars of laughter] I give him the most solemn pledge that I will to the very last stand by the law of this State, which forbids the marrying of white people with negroes. [Continued laughter and applause.]

Letter to Horace Greeley
August 22, 1862
Executive Mansion,
Washington

. . . I would save the Union. I would save it the shortest way under the Constitution. The sooner the national authority can be restored; the nearer the Union will be "the Union as it was." If there be those who would not save the Union, unless they could at the same time *save* slavery, I do not agree with them. If there be those who would not save the Union unless they could at the same time *destroy* slavery, I do not agree with them. My paramount object in this struggle *is* to save the Union without freeing *any* slave I would do it, and if I could save it by freeing *all* the slaves I would do it; and if I could save it by freeing some and leaving others alone I would also do that. What I do about slavery, and the colored race, I do because I believe it helps to save the Union; and what I forbear, I forbear because I do *not* believe it would help save the Union . . .

Questions for Discussion

1. What were you taught about Lincoln's views on race and slavery? Who made the decisions about what you would be taught?
2. Do these excerpts change your views of Lincoln in any way?
3. Do they change your views of the Civil War, or the relationship between the war and the end of slavery?

Blacks and the North

The Union army faced a manpower shortage. Many whites in the North refused to volunteer to serve in the army and some even defied the draft. Northern newspapers that were anti-Lincoln had misled the general white public to believe that the purpose of the war was to free the slaves (Franklin and Moss 1988, 186).

Blacks were universally despised in the North. Many counties and towns excluded blacks, and racial segregation existed in all areas of social life including jobs, education, and even in religious institutions. Only a few Northern white communities allowed blacks to vote. The very small number of blacks who did had to meet stringent criteria. Before and during the Civil War, the black community in the North was struggling for basic citizenship rights (Litwack 1961; Curry 1981).

Black Soldiers and the Emancipation Proclamation

Lincoln's military advisers and generals persuaded him to change the policy of returning runaway slaves to their masters and to use black men in the war. By doing this, they argued, the Southern economy, which was largely dependent on slave labor, would be severely undermined, and the Union army, with the addition of black soldiers, would become a more powerful and effective military force.

President Lincoln's famous Emancipation Proclamation, which many mistakenly believe is the act that freed the slaves, went into effect on January 1, 1863. It declared free all slaves in states or parts of states still in rebellion against the United States. However, these were areas where the Union army had no control. For instance, slaves in the border states of Missouri, Kentucky, Maryland, and Delaware that remained in the Union were not affected by the proclamation. Thus, in effect, Lincoln did not free one slave (Franklin 1988, 214–16).

Black people themselves were the principal force, which ended slavery. Over 186,000 black soldiers fought valiantly in the Civil War and more than 38, 000 lost their lives. It is estimated that their rate of mortality was about 40 percent greater than that among the white troops (Franklin and Moss 1988, 198–99).

Conclusion

To the detriment of black people, the reality that the myths about the United States are more widely known and believed than the historical facts points to the serious problem of miseducation. For these myths perpetuate and reinforce the racist idea that black people are incapable of doing things for themselves, and that they need a white savior to rescue or lead them. These mistaken ideas serve to make black people invisible while images portray them as pitiful inferior beings who need white help and guidance.

The great myths in American history are also an obstacle to racial harmony. They instill and foster patriotic feelings of righteousness and superiority in whites. These myths make whites less able to understand themselves and their society. Progress toward interracial harmony necessitates an assault on American chauvinism, which is largely a product of miseducation.

References

Barker, Lucius, and Jesse J. McCorry. 1980. *Black Americans and the Political System*. Cambridge, MA: Winthrop.

Bennett, Lerone. 1984. *Before the Mayflower*. New York, NY: Penguin.

Curry, Leonard P. 1981. *The Free Black in Urban America, 1800-1850*. Chicago: University of Chicago Press.

Dred Scott v. Sandford (60 U.S. 393. 19 How. 393. 1857).

Franklin, John H., and Alfred A. Moss. 1988. *From Slavery to Freedom: A History of Negro Americans*. New York: Knopf.

Franklin, John H. 1980. *From Slavery to Freedom: A History of Negro Americans*. New York: Knopf.

Fresia, Gerald J. 1988. *Toward an American Revolution: Exposing the Constitution and Other Illusions*. Boston, MA: South End Press.

Geschwender, James A. 1978. *Racial Stratification in America*. Dubuque, IA: W. C. Brown.

Litwack, Leon F. 1961. *North of Slavery: The Negro in the Free States, 1790-1860*. Chicago: University of Chicago Press.

McLemore, S. Dale. 1983. *Racial and Ethnic Relations in America*. Boston: Allyn and Bacon.

Questions for Discussion

1. Explain why you think that historians over generations have presented racial myths and distortions of race relations in textbooks.

2. Reflect on your K-12 educational experience. In your mind, did you question or disbelieve what you read in your textbooks on America as it related to racial equality?

3. Identify several racial myths, which perpetuate racism, that are currently fostered in American schools. Realistically, what can be done about it?

CHAPTER 7

Racial Ideological Warfare: IQ as a Weapon

Luke Tripp, Ph.D.

Introduction to the Article *IQ as a Weapon*

There is a widespread belief among some scholars and a large public that one's IQ determines one's location in the social hierarchy. The concept of innate intelligence is often used to explain and justify ones social position in the American stratification system. The fact that whites dominate the most powerful and privileged positions in society, disproportionate to their numbers, is often implicitly attributed to their alleged inherent superiority to other races in terms of intelligence, creativity, and morality. This article challenges the dominant American ideology of meritocracy and white supremacy and explains how the concept of IQ is used to justify the race and class structure and how it influences public social policy.

Many mainstream scholars attempt to camouflage the racist thrust of their analytical and conceptual framework by discussing social stratification in nonracial terms such as class, culture, and individual liberty to explain away or dismiss racial oppression. Regarding class, some argue that the racial patterns in residential areas and income disparity between blacks and whites can be explained completely by differences in socioeconomic status, even though blacks and whites of the same socioeconomic status tend to reside in separate areas. With respect to culture, they assert that blacks do not value education as much as whites and that black culture does not rather than do not strongly foster academic pursuits. For these reasons, they believe blacks are not well represented in the professional ranks. Individual liberty or free choice is often used to explain ones social location in the stratification system. The underlying assumption is that blacks as individuals choose unproductive or criminal life styles that cause them to end up in the lower strata of society.

Racial ideological warfare continues in America. This form of warfare is waged primarily against black people. A major force prosecuting this war is an array of white academics, scholars, intellectuals, and social scientists (Coughlin 1995; Heller 1994). Their major premise is that black people are mentally inferior to all other racial groups, especially the white race. This is the main thrust of *The Bell Curve: Intelligence and Class Structure in American Life* by Herrnstein and Murray which was ranked 5th on the New York Times Best Seller List on December 25, 1994. Its widespread popularity and appeal and the accelerated moves of American politics further to the right at all levels of government are concrete indications that America is becoming even more dangerous for black people.

Pseudo Science

Despite the fact that *The Bell Curve* is based on pseudo science, it should be taken seriously because its major themes fit nicely into the mainstream beliefs of whites and the implied messages of the dominant political forces. In this essay, we will examine the theories and concepts presented in *The Bell Curve*, and consider how they inform and rationalize a political agenda aimed at devaluing black people.

Herrnstein and Murray have attempted to present *The Bell Curve* as a scientific work by including voluminous studies on race and intelligence as if bulk and quantity were related to quality and validity. In their attempt to shield *The Bell Curve* from being labeled racist propaganda, which it is, they devote most of their book to the discussion of the relationship between IQ and social class rather than to the relationship between IQ and race. However, their principle message is clear: genetically, the *white race* is smarter than the *black race*.

Since race is a key causal variable in their hypothesis, we would expect them to rigorously define this variable; however, they failed to do this. In fact, they acknowledged that the categories used for the race variable were based on racial self-identification, not on the basis of some genetic criteria (DNA structure). Nevertheless, they used the concept of race as though it has some scientific validity and universal meaning. Omi and Winant (1986) note that the concept of race has defied biological definition and none of the ostensibly objective measures to determine and define racial categories have been free from the invidious elements of racial ideology. Furthermore, as Marshall (1993) emphasizes, scholars in the biological sciences agree that all topological divisions of humankind into discrete groups are to some extent artificial and arbitrary. She maintains that race has never been and will never be a primarily biological concept and concludes that race is a biopolitical concept, which serves to obfuscate the problems entailed in the study of human variation.

Much of the scholarly criticism of *The Bell Curve* has been directed at the weaknesses of the pseudo scientific research that Herrnstein and Murray used to support their theory that black people as a group are at the bottom of the stratified social structure in America because their cognitive ability is lower than that of other races. We will not review the body of research that they cited to support their assertions, nor will we ponder the debates about the validity and reliability of conventional IQ tests. Rather, we will focus on how the concept of IQ is used as a pseudo scientific scale to make invidious comparisons among the "races" and to disparage black people. We will also consider the effects of *The Bell Curve* on social policy and American politics.

Beliefs about Social Stratification

To determine the social and political effects of *The Bell Curve*, let us first examine the social ideology of white Americans. In general, what do white Americans believe about the nature of social stratification in America? Research studies show that most whites have been socialized to believe that America is (1) democratic, which implies that it is free of oppression, (2) meritocratic, which implies that a person's social location is determined by ability and effort, and (3) just, which implies that whatever unfortunate circumstances that may exist, they can be overcome, and that fair play is the rule, and privileges are earned (Huber and Form 1973).

In their study of beliefs about inequality, Kluegel and Smith (1986) found that a large majority of whites believe there is nearly equal educational and job opportunity. Whites believe one's socioeconomic status is determined by his/her individual attributes such as ability and effort. Another prevalent belief they hold is that economic inequality is necessary and beneficial. Moreover they endorse the idea of economic and societal equity as the just criteria for the distribution of income.

These basic beliefs constitute whites' ideological justification for socioeconomic inequality. Thus, for whites in general, the American class structure can be morally defended as a system which is fair because, although it is not based on the principle of equality, it does provide equal opportunity for success. Given these beliefs, they logically conclude that those who are at the bottom of the social structure are there because of some deficiencies in terms of ability and effort rather than other factors related to historic and continuing forms of oppression. These beliefs undergird the IQ based social stratification model presented in *The Bell Curve*.

Intelligence and Social Hierarchy

Herrnstein and Murray contend that cognitive ability primarily determines social location in America's stratified hierarchy, and they claim that IQ tests accurately measure cognitive ability. In their model the brightest are at the top of the social system and the dullards are at the bottom. They explain that this hierarchical pattern reflects the correspondence between the distribution of IQs and the distribution of socioeconomic rewards for the various levels of knowledge and skills, which range from the manual labor of an illiterate to the professional expertise of a neurosurgeon.

The underlying assumptions of *The Bell Curve* model are that (1) people will tend to seek high paying jobs; (2) there is fair competition for high paying jobs; (3) high paying jobs require a high IQ; (4) those with the highest IQs will get the highest paying jobs; and (5) the wealthiest are those with the highest IQs. We can see how this model is consistent with the way most whites believe the American social system operates, and thus, how IQ is used to explain and justify social stratification in America.

However, beliefs and facts are not necessarily the same thing. Social scientists have shown that peoples' social locations, especially among the upper social classes, are primarily based on their social and material inheritance, not their IQs. Furthermore, the inheritance of the upper social classes is largely derived from private capital and the ruthless exploitation of black people and the lower social classes. The American capitalist system precludes equal opportunity for the lower classes to compete for educational resources or jobs because the wealthy classes have systemic power and privileges. The point is that, in general, economic, social, and political power—rather than cognitive ability—primarily determines people's social positions.

Historical Perspective on Stratification and Race

At this point, we should consider the question of the determinants of social stratification in America in a historical context. From the first permanent English settlement in Jamestown Virginia, when in 1619 Africans were brought in chains to serve their white masters, to the present, blacks have been forcibly kept in a subordinate position in America. The dominant white ideology, which has historically justified and rationalized the superordinate position of whites and the subordinate position of blacks, is a set of white beliefs, which hold that black people are inherently inferior in terms of intelligence and morality and thus, they are unworthy of full human dignity and respect.

These beliefs served to defend slavery in America for about two and a half centuries and subsequently, to uphold legal racial segregation for another century, into the 1960s. The point is that an ideology of racism was used to justify a system of exploitation and oppression. Moreover, in America's social hierarchy, black peoples' subordinate social position was primarily determined by *race,* not by cognitive ability.

Racism and Psychological Processes

There are several psychological principles that may help us understand why the ideology of black inferiority remains entrenched in the culture, and the way in which *The Bell Curve* reinforces it. First, the principle of cognitive mastery holds that individuals attempt to understand their environments in order to enhance their social positions in them. This implies that they believe that their conscious actions can influence or determine outcomes. This leads to the general belief that people receive the outcomes they deserve. Thus, we see how this belief justifies social inequality.

Second, the socialization principle maintains that people come to believe what their society teaches them. Beliefs that are taught early and consistently enough form a basic framework of knowledge that is difficult for the individual to recognize. Racist beliefs permeate American society. They are taught in all areas of social life in America—home, school, church, workplace, and recreation. This explains why they are so pervasive.

Third, the principle of cognitive efficiency maintains that a discrete package of beliefs is retrieved from memory and guides inferences. For example, white racists are sensitive to the dimension of racial superiority in a wide range of situations, thus they disproportionately weight this dimension in making judgments and evaluations of social situations involving black people. Further, through associative links between concepts in memory (blacks and gangs, blacks and welfare, and blacks and crime), they engage in stereotypical thinking. With regard to *The Bell Curve*, the idea is fostered that blacks' low academic performance is linked to stupidity—not to the educational system's planned retardation of many ghetto-entrapped black children (Mazique 1992).

Fourth, principles regarding the relationship between affect and cognition imply that whites' feelings toward black people will influence their beliefs about black people. The white media, along with other institutions, have constructed enduring negative images of black people as comedic, criminal, dysfunctional, and dumb (Spigner 1991). These negative images of blacks foster negative feelings among whites, which condition them to believe any negative information about blacks. Thus, given the prevailing sentiments of whites, *The Bell Curve's* theme of black mental inferiority would seem quite credible to them.

Fifth, the hedonic principle holds that people seek to maintain high levels of self-esteem by attributing negative qualities to others, especially those unlike themselves. Richards (1992) asserts that the white self-image requires a negative image of black people in order to be positively reinforced. *The Bell Curve's* assertion of black intellectual inferiority definitely inflates whites' already vain ego and strengthens their self-image of racial superiority.

Last, the distributive justice principle holds that in some areas the idea of justice requires equality (equality under the law), in other areas equity (benefits should be distributed on the basis of ones' contribution), and under certain conditions, need may be the basis for distributive justice (the deserving poor should receive some benefits on the basis of need alone); however, in this connection, whites tend to view blacks on welfare as the undeserving poor.

Unfortunately, most whites have also been propagandized to believe that historic structural racial barriers have been virtually eliminated; therefore, they believe blacks have equal citizenship rights and opportunity. Many even believe that affirmative action policies discriminate against whites and thus, allow black people to have undeserved privileges and advantages, especially in higher education and the workplace. Consistent with the myth of equal, or near equal, opportunity for blacks is the false assumption found in *The Bell Curve* that there are few significant racial barriers to upward social mobility.

We can clearly see how *The Bell Curve* reinforces the prevailing white ideology of social inequality and taps into the widespread racial attitudes found among whites. The assertion that blacks have lower mental ability than whites has obvious appeal as an explanation for the lower socioeconomic status of blacks in a society that rewards intelligence. This help explains why *The Bell Curve* has such broad appeal among whites and why it represents a dangerous ideological attack on black people.

The Bell Curve and Politics

The political agenda of *The Bell Curve* is to eliminate affirmative action programs, defend the existing American class structure, and rationalize white domination and black subordination. *The Bell Curve* supports powerful antiblack political forces by providing them with an economic rationale for withdrawing governmental support for many programs that have, to some extent, benefited blacks, particularly in the area of education. Herrnstein and Murray assert that educational attainment gap between blacks and whites cannot be closed through educational enrichment programs for blacks because the gap is based on biology not sociology. They argue that programs that range from Head Start for preschoolers to Minority Opportunity Projects for college students are doomed to fail in their attempt to close the educational attainment gap between blacks and whites because this gap reflects a racial difference in IQ averages. Thus, they conclude that it is not cost effective to spend money for this effort.

They also provide right-wing political forces with spurious arguments against affirmation action policies, which they claim undermine the principle of reward on the basis of merit, and result in a lowering of quality standards in academia and the professions. This, they believe, will weaken America's competitiveness, and thus, have serious negative social and economic ramifications.

The political impact of *The Bell Curve* is especially significant in this period of intense anxiety about economic security and social mobility. Miller (1992) believes that America is in a "silent depression" characterized by slow economic growth, deteriorating living standards, and increasing economic inequality. Labor Secretary Robert Reich in his speech in January 1995 said that household incomes have swelled by $826 billion over the past 15 years, but that 98 percent of that increase has gone to the wealthiest (and most educated and skilled) fifth of Americans (Berg 1995).

Most Americans are facing the uncertain future with apprehension and foreboding. Increasing global competition and the so-called computer driven information age are the forces that are often cited as shaping the future economy of America, an economy that will demand higher cognitive ability and make low-skilled workers superfluous. These concrete economic conditions and trends provide a context for the politics of *The Bell Curve*.

Herrnstein and Murray argue that government policy should be designed to reward those with high IQs because they can make the greatest contribution to a rapidly developing hi-tech society. They believe that others with lower IQs deserve less attention; the group with the higher IQ is more deserving. In their Darwinian paradigm, cognitive ability is the criterion on which human beings are ranked, and the basis on which human worth is determined. Thus, IQ becomes a measure of human worth; it becomes the criterion for superiority (more rational, smarter, and more advanced).

Conclusion

The Bell Curve maintains and produces support for the existing race and class hierarchy. Herrnstein and Murray's IQ theory explain racial inequality as an inevitable feature of a stratified society based on IQ, which is genetically determined. They argue that black people's lower social position is the effect of their lower IQ in relation to whites, not the effect of racial oppression. By explaining the class structure in terms of ability (IQ), rather than in terms of white systemic power and control, they direct the analysis of social stratification away from the issue of class and racial domination.

They attempt to camouflage the racist thrust of *The Bell Curve* by discussing social stratification in nonracial terms (an IQ line rather than a color line). However, the logic of their pseudo science makes this virtually impossible. Their deterministic model is predicated on a casual relationship between biology and social class. Thus, according to their model, social IQ, which in turn is determined by genetics, which also defines race, determines class. Consequently, they cannot escape the contradiction of trying to make a racial point while denying that this was their intent (Wellman 1993).

The Bell Curve is another ideological in-your-face antiblack weapon wielded by the most reactionary sector of white intellectuals. Herrnstein, Murray, and their ilk represent the intellectual shock troops who dare articulate the enduring popular beliefs of white Americans, including the vast majority of white academics. Their main thesis of black mental inferiority is brutally to the point, but it is not new. For most of the history of American higher education, explicitly racist biological theories have been dominant among academics. Some of the most prominent and influential white American scholars have articulated and perpetuated a racist ideology based on the myth of black inferiority which is deeply rooted in the culture of academe (Harding 1993).

The political aims of *The Bell Curve* are to discredit key egalitarian ideas and to eliminate social programs ushered in by the black liberation movement. These aims are also strategic mobilizing elements in the political agenda of the increasingly aggressive Right wing. However, the Right wing has not yet loudly articulated the IQ thesis of *The Bell Curve*, probably because it is too explicitly racial. Even the most reactionary politicians prefer coded messages and more socially acceptable and politically expedient explanations for black and white inequality such as black's alleged "cultural deficiencies." Nevertheless, *The Bell Curve* reinforces white popular racial beliefs and strengthens the political undercurrents that are pushing American politics further to the right.

References

Berg, S. 1995. State of Insecurity. *Minneapolis Star Tribune*, January 22, A1.

Coughlin, E. K. 1995. Intelligence Researchers Issue Statement on Mainstream Science. *The Chronicle of Higher Education*, January 6, A15.

Harding, Sandra. 1993. "Eurocentric Scientific Illiteracy—A Challenge for the World Community." In *The Racial Economy of Science*, edited by Sandra Harding, 1–29. Bloomington, Indiana: University of Indiana Press.

Heller, Scott. 1994. At Conference, Conservative Scholars Lash Out at Attempts to Delegitimize Science. *The Chronicle of Higher Education*, November 23, A18.

Herrnstein, Richard J., and Charles A. Murray. 1994. *The Bell Curve: Intelligence and Class Structure in American Life*. New York: Free Press.

Huber, Joan, and William H. Form. 1973. *Income and Ideology*. New York: Free Press.

Kluegel, James R., and Eliot R. Smith. 1986. *Beliefs About Inequality*. Hawthorne, New York: Aldine de Gruyter.

Marshall, Gloria A. 1993. "Racial Classifications: Popular and Scientific." In *The Racial Economy of Science*, edited by Sandra Harding, 116–27. Bloomington, Indiana: University of Indiana Press.

Mazique, Jewell R.C. 1992. "Betrayal in the Schools." In *A Turbulent Voyage*, edited by Floyd W. Hayes, 468–75. San Diego, California: Collegiate Press.

Miller, J. 1992, April. Silent Depression: Economic Growth and Prosperity Part Company. *Dollars and Sense*, 6–9.

Omi, Michael, and Howard Winant. 1986. *Racial Formation in the United States*. New York: Routledge & Kegan Paul.

Richards, Donna. 1992. "The Ideology of Progress." In *A Turbulent Voyage,* edited by Floyd W. Hayes, 145–59. San Diego, California: Collegiate Press.

Spigner, Clarence. 1991. "Black Impressions of People-of-Color: A Functionalist Approach to Film Imagery." *The Western Journal of Black Studies,* 15: 69–78.

Wellman, David T. 1993. *Portraits of White Racism*. New York: Cambridge University Press.

Questions for Discussion

1. Studies show that whites tend to perceive racism as one of individual prejudice and acts of discrimination, and to believe that black and whites are treated equally in the workplace. Survey about 10 white people about these ideas and discuss their responses.

2. A substantial proportion of whites, believe that the lower socioeconomic status of blacks as compared with whites can be attributed to the lack of motivation of blacks and their innately inferior ability. Survey about 10 white people about these ideas and discuss their responses.

PART III

White Privilege, White Allies, White Choices

Jeanne A. Lacourt, Ph.D.

Introduction

Learning about white privilege can be challenging for some and confirming for others. Whether you are first learning to acknowledge what it is, or learning about historical policies that have advantaged whites over people of color, or feeling affirmed in how you and your ancestors have been treated as people of color in this country; learning about white privilege has the power to move us outside of our comfort zone. The articles in this section invite us to acknowledge that racial preference has a long established history in this country. They challenge people's reliance on the use of colorblindness as a response or solution to racism, and they offer alternative ways of engaging with race in the struggle to build an antiracist society.

Larry Adelman's article, "*A Long History of Racial Preference for Whites*" outlines a history of policies the United States has enacted that have granted privileges and advantages to whites. From replacing European indentured servants with African slaves to comparing net worth and assets accumulated over generations, Adelman spells out the rewards that come with the benefit of being white in the United States.

Lipsitz' article on "*The Possessive Investment of Whiteness*" examines the social/cultural construction of whiteness and points to the structural support for a long standing possessive investment in whiteness. Lipsitz shows us that the creation of whiteness came at the suffering of all racialized groups in this country: by slavery and segregation of Africans, by exclusion and low-wage immigrant labor from Asia and Mexico, and by the conquest and colonization of the indigenous people of the Americas. He also illustrates how government programs such as the Social Security Act, the Federal Housing Administration, and urban renewal have sanctioned and supported racism. Furthermore, Lipsitz explains how racial minority communities are exposed to greater health risks and are disproportionately represented in the criminal justice system. Although the Civil Rights Act of 1964 did help to reduce employment discrimination and lessen the gap between the rich and poor, attacks on the gains it has made has also proven to divide progressives along racial lines. Lipsitz argues that we cannot solely look at individual manifestations of discrimination and racism, we must also take into account the collective and coordinated group behaviors, and exercises of power, that create and perpetuate systemic racism today.

In Dottie Blais' "*The Perils of Color Blindness*," Blais shares with her readers a personal account that caused her to reflect on, and question, her own assumptions about colorblindness as a way of treating all her students as equals. As an educator, Blais came to understand the deceptive lure to "not see color" as a barrier to teaching and effectively communicating with her students. She acknowledges how *invisible* "others" become when we fail to *see* them.

Finally, Paul Kivel's work asks whites to take up the task of becoming a strong ally to people of color in an effort to end racism. Kivel provides examples of how whites both remain inactive—and thereby perpetuate racism when it occurs—and yet, how whites can also strategically address prejudice and racism in ways that disrupt it from happening time and again.

These articles, along with the popular and often referenced "*White Privilege: Unpacking the Invisible Knapsack*" by Peggy McIntosh (found easily by doing a Google search), ask us to acknowledge race in its many forms: from privilege and benefits, to how structures of power work to systemically disadvantage people of color. The challenge is ours. We must be uncomfortable with the current racialized system in this country. Can we be courageous enough to change, to move beyond our comfort, and to practice creating and modeling an antiracist society?

Questions for Discussion

1. What is your current comfort with acknowledging and talking about white privilege and how it works in your life? What makes it difficult or what enhances the discussion?

2. If you were to make an annotated timeline of United States policies that have systematically advantaged whites, what policies would appear on it and what advantages have whites gained because of these policies?

3. In what ways does the practice of using colorblindness obstruct our vision of equality?

4. Imagine yourself a "strong ally" right now. What would change in your current behaviors, opinions, and actions?

5. Read Peggy McIntosh's "White Privilege: Unpacking the Invisible Knapsack". Without reproducing any of her privileges, write three of your own. If you identify as a person of color, write three ways that you've been disadvantaged because of the color of your skin.

CHAPTER 8

A Long History of Racial Preferences—For Whites

Larry Adelman

Many middle-class white people, especially those of us who grew up in the suburbs, like to think we got to where we are today by virtue of our merit—hard work, intelligence, pluck, and maybe a little luck. And while we may be sympathetic to the plight of others, we close down when we hear the words "affirmative action" or "racial preferences." We worked hard, we made it on our own, the thinking goes, why don't 'they'? After all, it's been 40 years now since the Civil Rights Act was passed.

What we don't readily acknowledge is that racial preferences have a long, institutional history in this country—a white history. Here are a few ways in which government programs and practices have channeled wealth and opportunities to white people at the expense of others.

Early Racial Preferences

We all know the old history, but it's still worth reminding ourselves of its scale and scope. Affirmative action in the American "workplace" first began in the late seventeenth century when European indentured servants—the original source of unfree labor on the new tobacco plantations of Virginia and Maryland—were replaced by African slaves. Lower-class European settlers won new rights, entitlements, and opportunities from the planter elite in exchange for their support and their policing of the growing slave population.

White Americans were also given a head start with the help of the US Army. The 1830 Indian Removal Act, for example, forcibly relocated Cherokee, Creeks and other eastern Indians in what was called "The Trail of Tears" to west of the Mississippi River to make room for white settlers. The 1862 Homestead Act followed suit, giving away millions of acres—for free—of what had been Indian Territory west of the Mississippi. Ultimately, 270 million acres, or 10% of the total land area of the United States, was converted to private hands, overwhelmingly white, under Homestead Act provisions.

The 1790 Naturalization Act permitted only "free white persons" to become naturalized citizens, thus opening the doors to European immigrants but not others. Only citizens could vote, serve on juries, hold office, and in some cases, even hold property. In the twentieth century, Alien Land Laws passed in California and other states, reserved farm land for white growers by preventing Asian immigrants, ineligible to become citizens, from owning or leasing land. Immigration restrictions further limited opportunities for nonwhite groups. Racial barriers to naturalized US citizenship weren't removed until the McCarran-Walter Act in 1952, and white racial preferences in immigration remained in place until 1965.

In the South, the federal government never followed through on General Sherman's Civil War plan to divide up plantations and give each freed slave "40 acres and a mule" as reparations. Only once was monetary compensation made for slavery, That was in Washington, D.C. There, government officials paid up to $300 per slave upon emancipation—not to the slaves but to local slaveholders as compensation for the loss of their property.

When slavery ended, its legacy lived on not only in the impoverished condition of Black people but in the wealth and prosperity that accrued to white slaveowners and their descendants. Economists who try to place a dollar value on how much white Americans have profited from 200 years of unpaid slave labor, including interest, begin their estimates at $1 trillion.

Jim Crow laws, instituted in the late nineteenth and early twentieth centuries and not over-turned in many states until the 1960s, reserved the best jobs, neighborhoods, schools, and hospitals for white people for several more generations.

The Advantages Grow, Generation to Generation

Less known are more recent government racial preferences, first enacted during the New Deal, that directed wealth to white families and continue to shape life opportunities and chances today.

The landmark Social Security Act of 1935 provided a safety net for millions of workers, guaranteeing them an income after retirement. But the act specifically excluded two occupations: agricultural workers and domestic servants, who were predominately African American, Mexican, and Asian. As low-income workers, they also had the least opportunity to save for their retirement. They couldn't pass wealth on to their children. Just the opposite. During old age, their children had to support them.

Like Social Security, the 1935 Wagner Act helped establish an important new right for white people. By granting unions the power of collective bargaining, it helped millions of white workers gain entry into the middle class over the next 30 years. But the Wagner Act permitted unions to exclude non-whites and deny them access to better paid jobs and union protections and benefits such as health care, job security, and pensions. Many craft unions remained nearly all-white well into the 1970s. In 1972, for example, every single one of the 3,000 members of Los Angeles Steam Fitters Local #250 was still white.

But it was another racialized New Deal program, the Federal Housing Administration, that helped generate much of the wealth that so many white families enjoy today. These revolutionary programs made it possible for millions of average white Americans—but not others—to own a home for the first time. The government set up a notional neighborhood appraisal system, explicitly tying mortgage eligibility to race. Integrated communities were ipso facto deemed a financial risk, a policy known today as "redlining." Between 1934 and 1962, the federal government backed $120 billion of home loans, more than 98% went to whites. Of the 350,000 new homes built with federal support in northern California between 1946 and 1960, fewer than 100 went to African Americans.

These government programs made possible the new segregated white suburbs that sprang up around the country after World War II. Government subsidies for municipal services helped develop and enhance these suburbs further, in turn fueling commercial investments. New freeways tied the suburbs to central business districts, but they often cut through and destroyed the vitality of non-white neighborhoods in the central city.

Today, Black and Latino mortgage applicants are still 60% more likely than whites to be turned down for a loan, even after controlling for employment, financial, and neighborhood factors. According to the Census, whites are more likely to be segregated than any other group. As recently as 1993, 86% of suburban whites still lived in neighborhoods with a black population of less than 1%.

Reaping the Rewards of Racial Preference

One result of the generations of preferential treatment for whites is that a typical white family in 2005 has, on average, ten times the net worth of a typical African American family according to the US Census. Even when families of the same income are compared, white families have more than twice the wealth of Black families. Much of that wealth difference can be attributed to the value of one's home, and how much one inherited from parents.

But a family's net worth is not simply the finish line, it's also the starting point for the next generation. Those with wealth pass their assets on to their children—by financing a college education, lending a hand during hard times, or assisting with the down payment for a home. Some economists estimate that up to 80 percent of lifetime wealth accumulation depends on these inter-generational transfers. White advantage is passed down, from parent to child to grand-child. As a result, the racial wealth gap—and the head start enjoyed by whites—appears to have grown since the civil rights days.

In 1865, just after emancipation, it is not surprising that African Americans owned only 0.5 percent of the total worth of the United States. But by 1990, a full 135 years after the abolition of slavery, Black Americans still possessed only a meager 1 percent of national wealth. As legal scholar John A. Powell says in the documentary series *Race—The Power of an Illusion.* "The slick thing about whiteness is that whites are getting the spoils of a racist system even if they are not personally racist."

But rather than recognize how "racial preferences" have tilted the playing field and given as a head start in life, many whites continue to believe that race does not affect our lives. Instead, we chastise others for not achieving what we have; we even invert the situation and accuse non-whites of using "the race card" to advance themselves.

Or we suggest that differential outcomes may simply result from differences in "natural" ability or motivation. However, sociologist Dalton Conley's research shows that when we compare the performance of families across racial lines who make not just the same income, but also hold similar net worth, a very interesting thing happens: many of the racial disparities in education, graduation rates, welfare usage and other outcomes disappear. The "performance gap" between whites and nonwhites is a product not of unequal natures but unequal circumstances.

"Colorblind" policies that treat everyone the same, no exceptions for minorities, are often counter-posed against affirmative action. But colorblindness today merely bolsters the unfair advantages that color-coded practices have enabled white Americans to long accumulate.

Isn't it a little late in the game to suddenly decide that race shouldn't matter?

CHAPTER 9

The Possessive Investment in Whiteness

George Lipsitz

> Blacks are often confronted, in American life, with such devastating examples of the white descent from dignity; devastating not only because of the enormity of white pretensions, but because this swift and graceless descent would seem to indicate that white people have no principles whatever.
>
> —James Baldwin

Shortly after World War II, a French reporter asked expatriate Richard Wright for his views about the "Negro problem" in America. The author replied, "There isn't any Negro problem; there is only a white problem."[1] By inverting the reporter's question, Wright called attention to its hidden assumptions—that racial polarization comes from the existence of blacks rather than from the behavior of whites, that black people are a "problem" for whites rather than fellow citizens entitled to justice, and that, unless otherwise specified, "Americans" means "whites."[2] But Wright's formulation also placed political mobilization by African Americans during the civil rights era in context, connecting black disadvantages to white advantages and finding the roots of black consciousness in the systemic practices of aversion, exploitation, denigration, and discrimination practiced by people who think of themselves as "white."

Whiteness is everywhere in US culture, but it is very hard to see. As Richard Dyer suggests, "[W]hite power secures its dominance by seeming not to be anything in particular."[3] As the unmarked category against which difference is constructed, whiteness never has to speak its name, never has to acknowledge its role as an organizing principle in social and cultural relations.[4] To identify, analyze, and oppose the destructive consequences of whiteness, we need what Walter Benjamin called "presence of mind." Benjamin wrote that people visit fortune-tellers less out of a desire to know the future than out of a fear of not noticing some important aspect of the present. "Presence of mind," he suggested, "is an abstract of the future, and precise awareness of the present moment more decisive than foreknowledge of the most distant events."[5] In US society at this time, precise awareness of the present moment requires an understanding of the existence and the destructive consequences of the possessive investment in whiteness that surreptitiously shapes so much of our public and private lives."

Race is a cultural construct, but one with sinister structural causes and consequences. Conscious and deliberate actions have institutionalized group identity in the United States, not just through the dissemination of cultural stories, but also through systematic efforts from colonial times to the present to create economic advantages through a possessive investment in whiteness for

European Americans. Studies of culture too far removed from studies of social structure leave us with inadequate explanations for understanding racism and inadequate remedies for combating it.

Desire for slave labor encouraged European settlers in North America to view, first, Native Americans and, later, African Americans as racially inferior people suited "by nature" for the humiliating subordination of involuntary servitude. The long history of the possessive investment in whiteness stems in no small measure from the fact that all subsequent immigrants to North America have come to an already racialized society. From the start, European settlers in North America established structures encouraging a possessive investment in whiteness. The colonial and early national legal systems authorized attacks on Native Americans and encouraged the appropriation of their lands. They legitimated racialized chattel slavery, limited naturalized citizenship to "white" immigrants, identified Asian immigrants as expressly unwelcome (through legislation aimed at immigrants from China in 1882, from India in 1917, from Japan in 1924, and from the Philippines in 1934), and provided pretexts for restricting the voting, exploiting the labor, and seizing the property of Asian Americans, Mexican Americans, Native Americans, and African Americans.[6]

The possessive investment in whiteness is not a simple matter of black and white; all racialized minority groups have suffered from it, albeit to different degrees and in different ways. The African slave trade began in earnest only after large-scale Native American slavery proved impractical in North America. The abolition of slavery led to the importation of low-wage labor from Asia. Legislation banning immigration from Asia set the stage for the recruitment of low-wage labor from Mexico. The new racial categories that emerged in each of these eras all revolved around applying racial labels to "nonwhite" groups in order to stigmatize and exploit them while at the same time preserving the value of whiteness.

Although reproduced in new form in every era, the possessive investment in whiteness has always been influenced by its origins in the racialized history of the United States—by its legacy of slavery and segregation, of "Indian" extermination and immigrant restriction, of conquest and colonialism. Although slavery has existed in many countries without any particular racial dimensions to it, the slave system that emerged in North America soon took on distinctly racial forms. Africans enslaved in North America faced a racialized system of power that reserved permanent, hereditary, chattel slavery for black people. White settlers institutionalized a possessive investment in whiteness by making blackness synonymous with slavery and whiteness synonymous with freedom, but also by pitting people of color against one another. Fearful of alliances between Native Americans and African Americans that might challenge the prerogatives of whiteness, white settlers prohibited slaves and free blacks from traveling in "Indian country." European Americans used diplomacy and force to compel Native Americans to return runaway slaves to their white masters. During the Stono Rebellion of 1739, colonial authorities offered Native Americans a bounty for every rebellious slave they captured or killed. At the same time, British settlers recruited black slaves to fight against Native Americans within colonial militias.[7] The power of whiteness depended not only on white hegemony over separate racialized groups, but also on manipulating racial outsiders to fight against one another, to compete with each other for white approval, and to seek the rewards and privileges of whiteness for themselves at the expense of other racialized populations. . . .

Yet today the possessive investment is not simply the residue of conquest and colonialism, of slavery and segregation, of immigrant exclusion and "Indian" extermination. Contemporary whiteness and its rewards have been created and recreated by policies adopted long after the emancipation of slaves in the 1860s and even after the outlawing of *de jure* segregation in the 1960s. There has always been racism in the United States, but it has not always been the same racism. Political and cultural struggles over power have shaped the contours and dimensions of racism differently in different eras. . . .

Contemporary racism has been created anew in many ways over the past five decades, but most dramatically by the putatively race-neutral, liberal, social democratic reforms of the New Deal Era and by the more overtly race-conscious neoconservative reactions against liberalism since the Nixon years. It is a mistake to posit a gradual and inevitable trajectory of evolutionary progress in race relations; on the contrary, our history shows that battles won at one moment can later be lost. Despite hard-fought battles for change that secured important concessions during the 1960s in the form of civil rights legislation, the racialized nature of social policy in the United States since the Great Depression has actually increased the possessive investment in whiteness among European Americans over the past half century.

During the New Deal Era of the 1930s and 1940s, both the Wagner Act and the Social Security Act excluded farm workers and domestics from coverage, effectively denying those disproportionately minority sectors of the work force protections and benefits routinely afforded whites. The Federal Housing Act of 1934 brought home ownership within reach of millions of citizens by placing the credit of the federal government behind private lending to home buyers, but overtly racist categories in the Federal Housing Agency's (FHA) "confidential" city surveys and appraisers' manuals channeled almost all of the loan money toward whites and away from communities of color.[8] In the post-World War II era, trade unions negotiated contract provisions giving private medical insurance, pensions, and job security largely to the white workers who formed the overwhelming majority of the unionized work force in mass production industries, rather than fighting for full employment, medical care, and old-age pensions for all, or even for an end to discriminatory hiring and promotion practices by employers in those industries.[9]

Each of these policies widened the gap between the resources available to whites and those available to aggrieved racial communities. Federal housing policy offers an important illustration of the broader principles at work in the possessive investment in whiteness. By channeling loans away from older inner-city neighborhoods and toward white home buyers moving into segregated suburbs, the FHA and private lenders after World War II aided and abetted segregation in US residential neighborhoods. FHA appraisers denied federally supported loans to prospective home buyers in the racially mixed Boyle Heights neighborhood of Los Angeles in 1939, for example, because the area struck them as a "'melting pot' area literally honeycombed with diverse and subversive racial elements."[10] Similarly, mostly white St. Louis County secured five times as many FHA mortgages as the more racially mixed city of St. Louis between 1943 and 1960. Home buyers in the county received six times as much loan money and enjoyed per capita mortgage spending 6.3 times greater than those in the city.[11]

The federal government has played a major role in augmenting the possessive investment in whiteness. For years, the General Services Administration routinely channeled the government's own rental and leasing business to realtors who engaged in racial discrimination, while federally subsidized urban renewal plans reduced the already limited supply of housing for communities of color through "slum clearance" programs. In concert with FHA support for segregation in the suburbs, federal and state tax monies routinely funded the construction of water supplies and sewage facilities for racially exclusive suburban communities in the 1940s and 1950s. By the 1960s, these areas often incorporated themselves as independent municipalities in order to gain greater access to federal funds allocated for "urban aid."[12]

At the same time that FHA loans and federal highway building projects subsidized the growth of segregated suburbs, urban renewal programs in cities throughout the country devastated minority neighborhoods. During the 1950s and 1960s, federally assisted urban renewal projects destroyed 20 percent of the central-city housing units occupied by blacks, as opposed to only 10 percent of those inhabited by whites.[13] More than 60 percent of those displaced by urban renewal were African Americans, Puerto Ricans, Mexican Americans, or members of other minority racial groups.[14] The Federal Housing Administration and the Veterans Administration financed more than $120 billion worth of new housing between 1934 and 1962, but less than 2 percent of this real estate was available to nonwhite families—and most of that small amount was located in segregated areas.[15]

Even in the 1970s, after most major urban renewal programs had been completed, black central-city residents continued to lose housing units at a rate equal to 80 percent of what had been lost in the 1960s. Yet white displacement declined to the relatively low levels of the 1950s.[16] In addition, the refusal first to pass, then to enforce, fair housing laws has enabled realtors, buyers, and sellers to profit from racist collusion against minorities largely without fear of legal retribution. During the decades following World War II, urban renewal helped construct a new "white" identity in the suburbs by helping to destroy ethnically specific European American urban inner-city neighborhoods. Wrecking balls and bulldozers eliminated some of these sites, while others were transformed by an influx of minority residents desperately competing for a declining supply of affordable housing units. As increasing numbers of racial minorities moved into cities, increasing numbers of European American ethnics moved out. Consequently, ethnic differences among whites became a less important dividing line in US culture, while race became more important. The suburbs helped turn Euro-Americans into "whites" who could live near each other and intermarry with relatively little difficulty. But this "white" unity rested on residential segregation, on shared access to housing and life chances largely unavailable to communities of color.[17]

During the 1950s and 1960s, local "pro-growth" coalitions led by liberal mayors often justified urban renewal as a program designed to build more housing for poor people, but it actually destroyed more housing than it created. Ninety percent of the low-income units removed for urban renewal during the entire history of the program were never replaced. Commercial, industrial, and municipal projects occupied more than 80 percent of the land cleared for these projects, with less than 20 percent allocated for replacement housing. In addition, the loss of taxable properties and the tax abatements granted to new enterprises in urban renewal zones often meant serious tax increases for poor, working-class, and middle-class home owners and renters.[18] Although the percentage of black suburban dwellers also increased during this period, no significant desegregation of the suburbs took place. From 1960 to 1977, 4 million whites moved out of central cities, while the number of whites living in suburbs increased by 22 million; during the same years, the inner-city black population grew by 6 million, but the number of blacks living in suburbs increased by only 500,000.[19] By 1993, 86 percent of suburban whites still lived in places with a black population below 1 percent. At the same time, cities with large numbers of minority residents found themselves cut off from loans by the FHA. For example, because of their growing black and Puerto Rican populations, neither Camden nor Paterson, New Jersey, in 1966 received one FHA-sponsored mortgage.[20]

In 1968, lobbyists for the banking industry helped draft the Housing and Urban Development Act, which allowed private lenders to shift the risks of financing low-income housing to the government, creating a lucrative and thoroughly unregulated market for themselves. One section of the 1968 bill authorized FHA mortgages for inner-city areas that did not meet the usual eligibility criteria, and another section subsidized interest payments by low-income families. If administered wisely, these provisions might have promoted fair housing goals, but FHA administrators deployed them in ways that actually promoted segregation in order to provide banks, brokers, lenders, developers, realtors, and speculators with windfall profits. As a U.S. Commission on Civil Rights investigation later revealed, FHA officials collaborated with blockbusters in financing the flight of low-income whites out of inner-city neighborhoods, and then aided unscrupulous realtors and speculators by arranging purchases of substandard housing by minorities desperate to own their own homes. The resulting sales and mortgage foreclosures brought great profits to lenders (almost all of them white), but their actions led to price fixing and a subsequent inflation of housing costs in the inner city by more than 200 percent between 1968 and 1972. Bankers then foreclosed on the mortgages of thousands of these uninspected and substandard homes, ruining many inner-city neighborhoods. In response, the Department of Housing and Urban Development essentially red-lined inner cities, making them ineligible for future loans, a decision that destroyed the value of inner-city housing for generations to come.[21]

Federally funded highways designed to connect suburban commuters with downtown places of employment also destroyed already scarce housing in minority communities and often disrupted neighborhood life as well. Construction of the Harbor Freeway in Los Angeles, the Gulf Free-way in Houston, and the Mark Twain Freeway in St. Louis displaced thousands of residents and bisected neighborhoods, shopping districts, and political precincts. The processes of urban renewal and highway construction set in motion a vicious cycle: population loss led to decreased political power, which made minority neighborhoods more vulnerable to further urban renewal and freeway construction, not to mention more susceptible to the placement of prisons, incinerators, toxic waste dumps, and other projects that further depopulated these areas.

In Houston, Texas—where blacks make up slightly more than one quarter of the local population—more than 75 percent of municipal garbage incinerators and 100 percent of the city-owned garbage dumps are located in black neighborhoods.[22] A 1992 study by staff writers for the *National Law Journal* examined the Environmental Protection Agency's response to 1,177 toxic waste cases and found that polluters of sites near the greatest white population received penalties 500 percent higher than penalties imposed on polluters in minority areas—an average of $335,566 for white areas contrasted with $55,318 for minority areas. Income did not account for these differences—penalties for low-income areas on average actually exceeded those for areas with the highest median incomes by about 3 percent. The penalties for violating all federal environmental laws regulating air, water, and waste pollution were 46 percent lower in minority communities than in white communities. In addition, superfund remedies left minority communities waiting longer than white communities to be placed on the national priority list, cleanups that began from 12 to 42 percent later than at white sites, and with a 7 percent greater likelihood of "containment" (walling off a hazardous site) than cleanup, while white sites experienced treatment and cleanup 22 percent more often than containment.[23]

The federal Agency for Toxic Substances and Disease Registry's 1988 survey of children suffering from lead poisoning showed that among families with incomes under $6,000 per year, 36 percent of white children but 68 percent of black children suffered from excess lead in their bloodstreams. Among families with incomes above $15,000 per year, only 12 percent of white children but 38 percent of black children suffered from toxic levels of lead.[24] In the Los Angeles area, only 34 percent of whites inhabit areas with the most polluted air, but 71 percent of African Americans and 50 percent of Latinos live in neighborhoods with the highest levels of air pollution.[25] Nationwide, 60 percent of African Americans and Latinos live in communities with uncontrolled toxic waste sites.[26]

Scholarly studies reveal that even when adjusted for income, education, and occupational status, aggrieved racial minorities encounter higher levels of exposure to toxic substances than white people experience.[27] In 1987, the Commission for Racial Justice of the United Church of Christ found race to be the most significant variable in determining the location of commercial hazardous waste facilities.[28] In a review of sixty-four studies examining environmental disparities, the National Wildlife Federation found that racial disparities outnumbered disparities by income, and in cases where disparities in race and income were both present, race proved to be more important in twenty-two out of thirty tests.[29] As Robert D. Bullard demonstrates, "race has been found to be an independent factor, not reducible to class" in predicting exposure to a broad range of environmental hazards, including polluted air, contaminated fish, lead poisoning, municipal landfills, incinerators, and toxic waste dumps.[30] The combination of exposure to environmental hazards and employment discrimination establishes a sinister correlation between race and health. One recent government study revealed that the likelihood of dying from nutritional deficiencies was two and a half times greater among African Americans than among European Americans.[31] Another demonstrated that Asian and Pacific Islander recipients of aid for at-risk families exhibited alarming rates of stunted growth and underweight among children under the age of five.[32] Corporations systematically target Native American reservations when looking for locations for hazardous waste incinerators, solid waste landfills, and nuclear waste storage facilities; Navajo teenagers develop reproductive organ cancer at seventeen times the national average because of their exposure to radiation from uranium mines."[33] Latinos in East Los Angeles encounter some of the worst smog and the highest concentration of air toxins in southern California because of prevailing wind patterns and the concentration of polluting industries, freeways, and toxic waste dumps.[34] Environmental racism makes the possessive investment in whiteness literally a matter of life and death; if African Americans had access to the nutrition, wealth, health care, and protection against environmental hazards offered routinely to whites, seventy-five thousand fewer of them would die each year.[35]

Minorities are less likely than whites to receive preventive medical care or costly operations from Medicare. Eligible members of minority communities are also less likely than European Americans to apply for food stamps.[36] The labor of migrant farm workers from aggrieved racialized groups plays a vital role in providing adequate nutrition for others, but the farm workers and their children suffer disproportionately from health disorders caused by malnutrition.[37] In her important research on health policy and ethnic diversity, Linda Wray concludes that "the lower life expectancies for many ethnic minority groups and subgroups stem largely from their disproportionately higher rates of poverty, malnutrition, and poor health care."[38]

Just as residential segregation and urban renewal make minority communities disproportionately susceptible to health hazards, their physical and social location gives these communities a different relationship to the criminal justice system. A 1990 study by the National Institute on Drug Abuse revealed that while only 15 percent of the thirteen million habitual drug users in the United States were black and 77 percent were white, African Americans were four times more likely to be arrested on drug charges than whites in the nation as a whole, and seven to nine times more likely in Pennsylvania, Michigan, Illinois, Florida, Massachusetts, and New Jersey. A 1989 study by the Parents' Resource Institute for Drug Education discovered that African American high school students consistently showed lower levels of drug and alcohol use than their European American counterparts, even in high schools populated by residents of low-income housing projects. Yet, while comprising about 12 percent of the US population, blacks accounted for 10 percent of drug arrests in 1984, 40 percent in 1988, and 42 percent in 1990. In addition, white drug defendants receive considerably shorter average prison terms than African Americans convicted of comparable crimes. A U.S. Sentencing Commission study found in 1992 that half of the federal court districts that handled cases involving crack cocaine prosecuted minority defendants *exclusively*. A *Los Angeles Times* article in 1995 revealed that "black and Latino crack dealers are hammered with 10-year mandatory federal sentences while whites prosecuted in state court face a minimum of five years and often receive no more than a year in jail." Alexander Lichtenstein and Michael A. Kroll point out that sentences for African Americans in the federal prison system are 20 percent longer than those given to whites who commit the same crimes. They observe that if blacks received the same sentences as whites for these offenses, the federal prison system would require three thousand fewer prison cells, enough to close completely six of the new five-hundred bed institutions.[39]

Racial animus on the part of police officers, prosecutors, and judges accounts for only a small portion of the distinctive experience that racial minorities have with the criminal justice system. Economic devastation makes the drug trade appealing to some people in the inner city, while the dearth of capital in minority neighborhoods curtails opportunities for other kinds of employment. Deindustrialization, unemployment, and lack of intergenerational transfers of wealth undermine parental and adult authority in many neighborhoods. The complex factors that cause people to turn to drugs are no more prevalent in minority communities than elsewhere, but these communities and their inhabitants face more stress while having fewer opportunities to receive private counseling and treatment for their problems.

The structural weaknesses of minority neighborhoods caused by discrimination in housing, education, and hiring also play a crucial role in relations between inner-city residents and the criminal justice system. Cocaine dealing, which initially skyrocketed among white suburban residents, was driven into the inner city by escalating enforcement pressures in wealthy white communities. Ghettos and barrios became distribution centers for the sale of drugs to white suburbanites. Former New York and Houston police commissioner Lee Brown, head of the federal government's anti-drug efforts during the early years of the Clinton presidency and later mayor of Houston, noted, "There are those who bring drugs into the country. That's not the black community. Then you have wholesalers, those who distribute them once they get here, and as a rule that's not the black community. Where you find the blacks is in the street dealing."[40]

You also find blacks and other minorities in prison. Police officers in large cities, pressured to show results in the drive against drugs, lack the resources to effectively enforce the law everywhere (in part because of the social costs of deindustrialization and the tax limitation initiatives designed to shrink the size of government). These officers know that it is easier to make arrests and to secure convictions by confronting drug users in areas that have conspicuous street corner sales, that have more people out on the street with no place to go, and that have residents more likely to plead guilty and less likely to secure the services of attorneys who can get the charges against them dropped, reduced, or wiped off the books with subsequent successful counseling and rehabilitation. In addition, politicians supported by the public relations efforts of neoconservative foundations often portray themselves to suburban voters as opponents of the "dangerous classes" in the inner cities.

Minority disadvantages craft advantages for others. Urban renewal failed to provide new housing for the poor, but it played an important role in transforming the US urban economy from one that relied on factory production to one driven by producer services. Urban renewal projects subsidized the development of downtown office centers on previously residential land, and they frequently created buffer zones of empty blocks dividing poor neighborhoods from new shopping centers designed for affluent commuters. To help cities compete for corporate investment by making them appealing to high-level executives, federal urban aid favored construction of luxury housing units and cultural centers like symphony halls and art museums over affordable housing for workers. Tax abatements granted to these producer services centers further aggravated the fiscal crisis that cities faced, leading to tax increases on existing industries, businesses, and residences.

Workers from aggrieved racial minorities bore the brunt of this transformation. Because the 1964 Civil Rights Act came so late, minority workers who received jobs because of it found themselves more vulnerable to seniority-based layoffs when businesses automated or transferred operations overseas. Although the act initially made real progress in reducing employment discrimination, lessened the gaps between rich and poor and between black and white workers, and helped bring minority poverty to its lowest level in history in 1973, that year's recession initiated a reversal of minority progress and a reassertion of white privilege.[41] In 1977, the U.S. Civil Rights Commission reported on the disproportionate impact of layoffs on minority workers. In cases where minority workers made up only 10 to 12 percent of the work force in their area, they accounted for from 60 to 70 percent of those laid off in 1974. The principle of seniority, a trade union triumph designed to protect workers from age discrimination, in this case guaranteed that minority workers would suffer most from technological changes, because the legacy of past discrimination by their employers left them with less seniority than white workers.[42]

When housing prices increased dramatically during the 1970s, white home owners who had been able to take advantage of discriminatory FHA financing policies in the past realized increased equity in their homes, while those excluded from the housing market by earlier policies found themselves facing even higher costs of entry into the market in addition to the traditional obstacles presented by the discriminatory practices of sellers, realtors, and lenders. The contrast between European Americans and African Americans is instructive in this regard. Because whites have access to broader housing choices than blacks, whites pay 15 percent less than blacks for similar housing in the same neighborhood. White neighborhoods typically experience housing costs 25 percent lower than would be the case if the residents were black.[43]

A recent Federal Reserve Bank of Boston study revealed that Boston bankers made 2.9 times as many mortgage loans per 1,000 housing units in neighborhoods inhabited by low-income whites than in neighborhoods populated by low-income blacks.[44] In addition, loan officers were far more likely to overlook flaws in the credit records of white applicants or to arrange creative financing for them than they were with black applicants.[45] A Los Angeles study found that loan officers more frequently used dividend income and underlying assets as criteria for judging black applicants than for whites.[46] In Houston, the NCNB Bank of Texas disqualified 13 percent of middle-income white loan applicants but 36 percent of middle-income black applicants.[47] Atlanta's home loan institutions gave five times as many home loans to whites as to blacks in the late 1980s. An analysis of sixteen Atlanta neighborhoods found that home buyers in white neighborhoods received conventional financing four times as often as those in black sections of the city.[48] Nationwide, financial institutions receive more money in deposits from black neighborhoods than they invest in them in the form of home mortgage loans, making home lending a vehicle for the transfer of capital away from black savers toward white investors.[49] In many locations, high-income blacks were denied loans more often than low-income whites.[50]

When confronted with evidence of systematic racial bias in home lending, defenders of the possessive investment in whiteness argue that the disproportionate share of loan denials to members of minority groups stems not from discrimination, but from the low net worth of minority applicants, even those who have high incomes. This might seem a reasonable position, but net worth is almost totally determined by past opportunities for asset accumulation, and therefore is the one figure most likely to reflect the history of discrimination. Minorities are told, in essence, "We can't give you a loan today because we've discriminated against members of your race so effectively in the past that you have not been able to accumulate any equity from housing and to pass it down through the generations."

Most white families have acquired their net worth from the appreciation of property that they secured under conditions of special privilege in a discriminatory housing market. In their prize-winning book *Black Wealth/White Wealth,* Melvin Oliver and Thomas Shapiro demonstrate how the history of housing discrimination makes white parents more able to borrow funds for their children's college education or to loan money to their children to enter the housing market. In addition, much discrimination in home lending is not based on considerations of net worth; it stems from decisions made by white banking officials based on their stereotypes about minority communities. The Federal Reserve Bank of Boston study showed that black and Latino mortgage applicants are 60 percent more likely to be turned down for loans than whites, even after controlling for employment, financial, and neighborhood characteristics.[51] Ellis Cose reports on a white bank official confronted with evidence at a board of directors' meeting that his bank denied loans to blacks who had credit histories and earnings equal to those of white applicants who received loans. The banker replied that the information indicated that the bank needed to do a better job of "affirmative action," but one of his colleagues pointed out that the problem had nothing to do with affirmative action—the bank was simply letting prejudice stand in the way of its own best interests by rejecting loans that should be approved.[52]

Yet bankers also make money from the ways in which discrimination creates artificial scarcities in the market. Minorities have to pay more for housing because much of the market is off limits to them. Blockbusters profit from exploiting white fears and provoking them into panic selling. Minority home owners denied loans in mainstream banks often turn to exploitative lenders who make "low end" loans at enormously high interest rates. If they fail to pay back these loans, regular banks can acquire the property cheaply and charge someone else exorbitant interest for a loan on the same property.

Federal home loan policies have put the power of the federal government at the service of private discrimination. Urban renewal and highway construction programs have enhanced the possessive investment in whiteness directly through government initiatives. In addition, decisions about where to locate federal jobs have also systematically subsidized whiteness. Federal civilian employment dropped by 41,419 in central cities between 1966 and 1973, but total federal employment in metropolitan areas grew by 26,558.[53] While one might naturally expect the location of government buildings that serve the public to follow population trends, the federal government's policy of locating offices and records centers in suburbs aggravated the flight of jobs to suburban locations less accessible to inner-city residents. Because racial discrimination in the private sector forces minority workers to seek government positions disproportionate to their numbers, these moves exact particular hardships on them. In addition, minorities who follow their jobs to the suburbs must generally allocate more for commuter costs, because housing discrimination makes it harder and more expensive for them than for whites to relocate.

The policies of neoconservatives in the Reagan and Bush administrations during the 1980s and 1990s greatly exacerbated the racialized aspects of more than fifty years of these social welfare policies. Regressive policies that cut federal aid to education and refused to challenge segregated education, housing, and hiring, as well as the cynical cultivation of an antiblack consensus through attacks on affirmative action and voting rights legislation clearly reinforced possessive investments in whiteness. In the US economy, where 86 percent of available jobs do not appear in classified ads and where personal connections prove the most important factor in securing employment, attacks on affirmative action guarantee that whites will be rewarded for their historical advantage in the labor market rather than for their individual abilities or efforts.[54]

Attacking the civil rights tradition serves many functions for neoconservatives. By mobilizing existing racisms and generating new ones, neoconservatives seek to discredit the egalitarian and democratic social movements of the post-World War II era and to connect the attacks by those movements on wealth, special privilege, and elite control over education and opportunity to despised and unworthy racial "others."

Attacks on the gains made by civil rights activism also act as a wedge to divide potentially progressive coalitions along racial lines, a strategy that attained its peak moment with the defection of "blue collar" trade unionists from the Democratic Party in the 1980s to become "Reagan Democrats." In addition to protecting centralized power and wealth and dividing its opponents, the neoracism of contemporary conservatism also functions as an important unifying symbol for a disparate and sometimes antagonistic coalition that includes Hamiltonian big-government conservatives as well as antistate libertarians, and that incorporates born-again Christians into an alliance with "objectivist" free market thinkers who celebrate selfishness and view the love of gain as the engine of human progress. This coalition often has trouble agreeing on the things it favors, but it has no difficulty agreeing about the alleged bad behavior and inferior morality of minority individuals and communities. Most important, by generating an ever repeating cycle of "moral panics" about the family, crime, welfare, race, and terrorism, neoconservatives produce a perpetual state of anxiety that obscures the actual failures of conservatism as economic and social policy, while promoting demands for even more draconian measures of a similar nature for the future. The neoracism of contemporary conservatism plays a vital role in building a countersubversive consensus because it disguises the social disintegration brought about by neoconservatism itself as the fault of "inferior" social groups, and because it builds a sense of righteous indignation among its constituents that enables them to believe that the selfish and self-interested politics they pursue are actually part of a moral crusade.

Yet even seemingly race-neutral policies supported by both neoconservatives and liberals in the 1980s and 1990s have increased the absolute value of being white. In the 1980s, changes in federal tax laws decreased the value of wage income and increased the value of investment income—a move harmful to minorities, who suffer from a gap between their total wealth and that of whites even greater than the disparity between their income and white income. The failure to raise the minimum wage between 1981 and 1989 and the decline of more than one-third in the value of Aid to Families with Dependent Children (AFDC) payments injured all poor people, but they exacted special costs on nonwhites, who faced even more constricted markets for employment, housing, and education than poor whites.[55]

Similarly, the "tax reforms" of the 1980s made the effective rate of taxation higher on investment in actual goods and services than on profits from speculative enterprises. This change encouraged the flight of capital from industrial production with its many employment opportunities toward investments that can be turned over quickly to allow the greatest possible tax write-offs. Government policies thus discouraged investments that might produce high-paying jobs and encouraged investors to strip companies of their assets to make rapid short-term profits. These policies hurt almost all workers, but they fell particularly heavily on minority workers, who because of employment discrimination in the retail and small business sectors were overrepresented in blue-collar industrial jobs.

On the other hand, while neoconservative tax policies created incentives for employers to move their enterprises elsewhere, they created disincentives for home owners to move. Measures like California's Proposition 13 (passed in 1978) granting tax relief to property owners badly misallocate housing resources, because they make it financially unwise for the elderly to move out of large houses, further reducing the supply of housing available to young families. While one can well understand the necessity for protecting senior citizens on fixed incomes from tax increases that would make them lose their homes, the rewards and punishments provided by Proposition 13 are so extreme that they prevent the kinds of generational succession that have routinely opened up housing to young families in the past. This reduction works particular hardships on those who also face discrimination by sellers, realtors, and lending institutions.

Subsidies to the private sector by government agencies also tend to enhance the rewards of past discrimination. Throughout the country, tax increment financing for redevelopment programs offers tax-free and low-interest loans to developers whose projects use public services, often without having to pay taxes to local school boards or county governments. In St. Louis, for example, tax abatements for wealthy corporations deprive the city's schools (and their majority African American population) of $17 million a year. Even if these redevelopment projects eventually succeed in increasing municipal revenues through sales and earnings taxes, their proceeds go to funds that pay for the increased services these developments demand (fire and police protection, roads, sewers, electricity, lighting, etc.) rather than to school funds, which are dependent upon property tax revenues.[56] Nationwide, industrial development bonds resulted in a $7.4 billion tax loss in 1983, which ordinary taxpayers had to make up through increased payroll taxes. Compared to white Americans, people of color, more likely to be poor or working class, suffer disproportionately from these changes as taxpayers, as workers, and as tenants. A study by the Citizens for Tax Justice found that wealthy Californians spend less than eleven cents in taxes for every dollar earned, while poor residents of the state pay fourteen cents out of every dollar in taxes. As groups overrepresented among the poor, minorities have been forced to subsidize the tax breaks given to the wealthy.[57] While holding property tax assessments for businesses and some home owners to about half of their market value, California's Proposition 13 deprived cities and counties of $13 billion a year in taxes. Businesses alone avoided $3.3 billion to $8.6 billion in taxes per year under this statute.[58]

Because they are ignorant of even the recent history of the possessive investment in whiteness—generated by slavery and segregation, immigrant exclusion and Native American policy, conquest and colonialism, but augmented by liberal and conservative social policies as well—Americans produce largely cultural explanations for structural social problems. The increased possessive investment in whiteness generated by disinvestment in US cities, factories, and schools since the 1970s disguises as *racial* problems, the general social problems posed by deindustrialization, economic restructuring, and neoconservative attacks on the welfare state. It fuels a discourse that demonizes people of color for being victimized by these changes, while hiding the privileges of whiteness by attributing the economic advantages enjoyed by whites to their family values, faith in fatherhood, and foresight—rather than to the favoritism they enjoy through their possessive investment in whiteness.

The demonization of black families in public discourse since the 1970s is particularly instructive in this regard. During the 1970s, the share of low-income households headed by blacks increased by one-third, while black family income fell from 60 percent of white family income in 1971 to 58 percent in 1980. Even adjusting for unemployment and for African American disadvantages in life-cycle employment (more injuries, more frequently interrupted work histories, confinement to jobs most susceptible to layoffs), the wages of full-time year-round black workers fell from 77 percent of white workers' income to 73 percent by 1986. In 1986, white workers with high school diplomas earned $3,000 per year more than African Americans with the same education.[59] Even when they had the same family structure as white workers, blacks found themselves more likely to be poor.

Recent economic gains by blacks brighten the picture somewhat, but the deindustrialization and economic restructuring of the 1970s and 1980s imposes yet another racial penalty on wage earners from minority communities, who suffered setbacks while members of other groups accumulated equity-producing assets. And even when some minority groups show improvement, others do not. In 1995, for example, every US ethnic and racial group experienced an increase in income except the twenty-seven million Hispanics, who experienced a 5.1 percent drop in income during that year alone.[60]

Forty-six percent of black workers between the ages of twenty and twenty-four held blue-collar jobs in 1976, but only 20 percent by 1984. Earnings by young black families that had reached 60 percent of white families' income in 1973, fell to 46 percent by 1986. Younger African American families experienced a 50 percent drop in real earnings between 1973 and 1986, with the decline in black male wages particularly steep.[61] Many recent popular and scholarly studies have delineated the causes for black economic decline over the past two decades.[62] Deindustrialization has decimated the industrial infrastructure that formerly provided high wage jobs and chances for upward mobility to black workers. Neoconservative attacks on government spending for public housing, health, education, and transportation have deprived members of minority groups of needed services and opportunities for jobs in the public sector. A massive retreat at the highest levels of government from the responsibility to enforce antidiscrimination laws has sanctioned pervasive overt and covert racial discrimination by bankers, realtors, and employers.

Yet public opinion polls of white Americans reflect little recognition of these devastating changes. Seventy percent of whites in one poll said that African Americans "have the same opportunities to live a middle-class life as whites," and nearly three-fourths of white respondents to a 1989 poll believed that opportunities for blacks had improved under Reagan.[63] If such optimism about the opportunities available to African Americans does not demonstrate ignorance of the dire conditions facing black communities, it indicates that many whites believe that blacks suffer deservedly, because they do not take advantage of the opportunities offered them. In opinion polls, favorable assessments of black chances for success often accompanied extremely negative judgments about the abilities, work habits, and character of black people. A National Opinion Research Report in 1990 disclosed that more than 50 percent of US whites viewed blacks as innately lazy and less intelligent and less patriotic than whites.[64] More than 60 percent said that they believed that blacks suffer from poor housing and employment opportunities because of their own lack of will power. Some 56.3 percent said that blacks preferred welfare to employment, while 44.6 percent contended that blacks tended toward laziness.[65] Even more important, research by Mary Edsall and Thomas Byrne Edsall indicates that many whites structure nearly all of their decisions about housing, education, and politics in response to their aversions to black people.[66]

The present political culture in this country gives broad sanction for viewing white supremacy and antiblack racism as forces from the past, as demons finally put to rest by the passage of the 1964 Civil Rights Act and the 1965 Voting Rights Act.[67] Jurists, journalists, and politicians have generally been more vocal in opposing what they call "quotas" and "reverse discrimination"—by which they usually mean race-specific measures, designed to remedy existing racial discrimination, that inconvenience or offend whites—than in challenging the thousands of well-documented cases every year of routine, systematic, and unyielding discrimination against minorities. It is my contention that the stark contrast between nonwhite experiences and white opinions during the past two decades cannot be attributed solely to individual ignorance or intolerance, but stems instead from liberal individualism's inability to describe adequately the collective dimensions of our experience.[68] As long as we define social life as the sum total of conscious and deliberative individual activities, we will be able to discern as racist only *individual* manifestations of personal prejudice and hostility. Systemic, collective, and coordinated group behavior consequently drops out of sight. Collective exercises of power that relentlessly channel rewards, resources, and opportunities from one group to another will not appear "racist" from this perspective, because they rarely announce their intention to discriminate against individuals. Yet they nonetheless give racial identities their sinister social meaning by giving people from different races vastly different life chances.

The gap between white perception and minority experience can have explosive consequences. Little more than a year after the 1992 Los Angeles rebellion, a sixteen-year-old high school junior shared her opinions with a reporter from the *Los Angeles Times*. "I don't think white people owe anything to black people," she explained. "We didn't sell them into slavery, it was our ancestors. What they did was wrong, but we've done our best to make up for it." A seventeen-year-old senior echoed those comments, telling the reporter, "I feel we spend more time in my history class talking about what whites owe blacks than just about anything else when the issue of slavery comes up. I often received dirty looks. This seems strange given that I wasn't even alive then. And the few members of my family from that time didn't have the luxury of owning much, let alone slaves. So why, I ask you, am I constantly made to feel guilty?"[69]

More ominously, after pleading guilty to bombing two homes and one car, vandalizing a synagogue, and attempting to start a race war by planning the murder of Rodney King and the bombing of Los Angeles's First African Methodist Episcopal Church, twenty-year-old Christopher David Fisher explained that "sometimes whites were picked on because of the color of their skin. . . . Maybe we're blamed for slavery."[70] Fisher's actions were certainly extreme, but his justification of them drew knowingly and precisely on a broadly shared narrative about the victimization of "innocent" whites by irrational and ungrateful minorities.

The comments and questions raised about the legacy of slavery by these young whites illuminate broader currents in our culture, with enormous implications for understanding the enduring significance of race in our country. These young people associate black grievances solely with slavery, and they express irritation at what they perceive as efforts to make them feel guilty or unduly privileged because of things that happened in the distant past. The claim that one's own family did not own any slaves is frequently voiced in our culture. It is almost never followed with a statement to the effect that of course some people's families did own slaves and we will not rest until we track them down and make them pay reparations. This view never acknowledges how the existence of slavery and the exploitation of black labor after emancipation created opportunities from which immigrants and others benefited, even if they did not personally own slaves. Rather, it seems to hold that, because not all white people owned slaves, no white people can be held accountable or inconvenienced by the legacy of slavery. More important, having dispensed with slavery, they feel no need to address the histories of Jim Crow segregation, racialized social policies, urban renewal, or the revived racism of contemporary neoconservatism. On the contrary, Fisher felt that his discomfort with being "picked on" and "blamed" for slavery gave him good reason to bomb homes, deface synagogues, and plot to kill black people.

Unfortunately for our society, these young whites accurately reflect the logic of the language of liberal individualism and its ideological predispositions in discussions of race. In their apparent ignorance of the disciplined, systemic, and collective *group* activity that has structured white identities in US history, they are in good company. In a 1979 law journal article, future Supreme Court Justice Antonin Scalia argued that affirmative action "is based upon concepts of racial indebtedness and racial entitlement rather than individual worth and individual need" and is thus "racist."[71] Yet liberal individualism is not completely color-blind on this issue. As Cheryl I. Harris demonstrates, the legacy of liberal individualism has not prevented the Supreme Court from recognizing and protecting the group interests of *whites* in the Bakke, Croson, and Wygant cases.[72] In each case, the Court nullified affirmative action programs because they judged efforts to help blacks as harmful to whites: to white expectations of entitlement, expectations based on the possessive investment in whiteness they held as members of a group. In the Bakke case, for instance, where the plaintiff argued that medical school affirmative action programs disadvantaged white applicants like himself, neither Bakke nor the Court contested the legitimacy of medical school admissions standards that reserved five seats in each class for children of wealthy donors to the university or that penalized Bakke for being older than most of the other applicants. The group rights of not-wealthy people or of people older than their classmates did not compel the Court or Bakke to make any claim of harm. But they did challenge and reject a policy designed to offset the effects of past and present discrimination when they could construe the medical school admission policies as detrimental to the interests of whites as a group—and as a consequence they applied the "strict scrutiny" standard to protect whites while denying that protection to people of color. In this case, as in so many others, the language of liberal individualism serves as a cover for coordinated collective group interests.

Group interests are not monolithic, and aggregate figures can obscure serious differences within racial groups. All whites do not benefit from the possessive investment in whiteness in precisely the same ways; the experiences of members of minority groups are not interchangeable. But the possessive investment in whiteness always affects individual and group life chances and opportunities. Even in cases where minority groups secure political and economic power through collective mobilization, the terms and conditions of their collectivity and the logic of group solidarity are always influenced and intensified by the absolute value of whiteness in US politics, economics, and culture.[73]

In the 1960s, members of the Black Panther Party used to say that "if you're not part of the solution, you're part of the problem." But those of us who are "white" can only become part of the solution if we recognize the degree to which we are already part of the problem—not because of our race, but because of our possessive investment in it. Neither conservative "free market" policies nor liberal social welfare policies can solve the "white problem" in the United States, because both reinforce the possessive investment in whiteness. . . .

Failure to acknowledge our society's possessive investment in whiteness prevents us from facing the present openly and honestly. It hides from us the devastating costs of disinvestment in America's infrastructure over the past two decades and keeps us from facing our responsibility to reinvest in human resources by channeling resources toward education, health, and housing—and away from subsidies for speculation and luxury. After two decades of disinvestment, the only further disinvestment we need is from the ruinous pathology of whiteness, which has always undermined our own best instincts and interests.

Notes

The epigraph is from Baldwin, *The Devil Finds Work,* 1.

1. Raphael Tardon, "Richard Wright Tells Us: The White Problem in the United States," *Action,* October 24, 1946. Reprinted in Kenneth Kinnamon and Michel Fabre, *Conversations with Richard Wright* (Jackson: University Press of Mississippi, 1993), 99. Malcolm X and others used this same formulation in the 1960s, but I believe that it originated with Wright, or at least that is the earliest citation I have found.

2. Toni Morrison points out the ways in which African Americans play an essential role in the white imagination, how their representations both hide and reveal the terms of white supremacy upon which the nation was founded and has been sustained ever since. See *Playing in the Dark: Whiteness in the Literary Imagination* (Cambridge: Harvard University Press, 1992).

3. Richard Dyer, "White," *Screen* 29, 4 (fall 1998): 44.

4. I thank Michael Schudson for pointing out to me that since the passage of civil rights legislation in the 1960s whiteness dares not speak its name, cannot speak in its own behalf, but rather advances through a color-blind language radically at odds with the distinctly racialized distribution of resources and life chances in US society.

5. Walter Benjamin, "Madame Ariane: Second Courtyard on the Left," in *One-Way Street* (London: New Left Books, 1969), 98–99.

6. See Lisa Lowe, *Immigrant Acts: On Asian American Cultural Politics* (Durham, NC: Duke University Press, 1996), 11–16; Gary B. Nash, *Red, White, and Black: The Peoples of Early America* (Englewood Cliffs, NJ: Prentice-Hall, 1974); Ronald Takaki, *A Different Mirror: A History of Multicultural America* (Boston: Little, Brown, 1993), 177–83.

7. Nash, *Red, White, and Black,* 292–93.

8. See Kenneth Jackson, *Crabgrass Frontier: The Suburbanization of the United States* (New York: Oxford University Press, 1985), and Douglas S. Massey and Nancy A. Denton, *American Apartheid: Segregation and the Making of the Underclass* (Cambridge: Harvard University Press, 1993).

9. I thank Phil Ethington for pointing out to me that these aspects of New Deal policies emerged out of political negotiations between the segregationist Dixiecrats and liberals from the North and West. My perspective is that white supremacy was not a gnawing aberration within the New Deal coalition but rather an essential point of unity between southern whites and northern white ethnics.

10. Records of the Federal Home Loan Bank Board of the Home Owners Loan Corporation, City Survey File, Los Angeles, 1939, Neighborhood D-53, National Archives, Box 74, RG 195.

11. Massey and Denton, *American Apartheid,* 54.

12. John R. Logan and Harvey Molotch, *Urban Fortunes: The Political Economy of Place* (Berkeley and Los Angeles: University of California Press, 1987), 182.

13. Ibid., 114.

14. Arlene Zarembka, *The Urban Housing Crisis: Social, Economic, and Legal Issues and Proposals* (Westport, CT: Greenwood, 1990), 104.

15. Jill Quadagno, *The Color of Welfare: How Racism Undermined the War on Poverty* (New York: Oxford University Press, 1994), 92, 91.

16. Logan and Molotch, *Urban Fortunes,* 130.

17. See Gary Gerstle, "Working-Class Racism: Broaden the Focus," *International Labor and Working Class History* 44 (fall 1993): 36.

18. Logan and Molotch, *Urban Fortunes,* 168–69.

19. Troy Duster, "Crime, Youth Unemployment, and the Underclass," *Crime and Delinquency* 33, 2 (April 1987): 308, 309.

20. Massey and Denton, *American Apartheid,* 55.

21. Quadagno, *The Color of Welfare,* 105, 113; Massey and Denton, *American Apartheid,* 204–5.

22. Logan and Molotch, *Urban Fortunes,* 113.

23. Robert D. Bullard, "Environmental Justice for All," in *Unequal Protection: Environmental Justice and Communities of Color,* ed. Robert Bullard (San Francisco: Sierra Club, 1994), 9–10.

24. Robert D. Bullard, "Anatomy of Environmental Racism and the Environmental Justice Movement," in *Confronting Environmental Racism: Voices from the Grass Roots,* ed. Robert D. Bullard (Boston: South End, 1993), 21.

25. Bullard, "Environmental Justice for All," 13.

26. Charles Lee, "Beyond Toxic Wastes and Race," in *Confronting Environmental Racism: Voices from the Grass Roots,* ed. Robert D. Bullard (Boston: South End, 1993), 49. Two corporate-sponsored research institutes challenged claims of racial bias in the location and operation of toxic and hazardous waste systems. Andy B. Anderson, Douglas L. Anderton, and John Michael Oakes made the corporate case in "Environmental Equity: Evaluating TSDF Siting over the Past Two Decades," *Waste Age,* July 1994. These results were trumpeted in a report by the Washington University Center for the Study of

American Business, funded by the John M. Olin Foundation. But the study by Anderson, Anderton, and Oakes was sponsored by the Institute of Chemical Waste Management, an industry trade group. The researchers claimed that their results were not influenced by corporate sponsorship, but they limited their inquiry to urban areas with toxic storage, disposal, and treatment facilities, conveniently excluding seventy facilities, 15 percent of TSDFs, and 20 percent of the population. The world's largest waste company, WMX Company, contributed $250,000 to the study, and the study's research plan excluded from scrutiny two landfills owned by WMX: the nation's largest commercial landfill, located in the predominately African American city of Emelle, Alabama, and the nation's fifth largest landfill, in Kettelman City Hills, California, a predominately Latino community.

27. Bunyan Bryant and Paul Mohai, *Race and the Incidence of Environmental Hazards* (Boulder, CO: Westview, 1992).
28. Lee, "Beyond Toxic Wastes and Race," 48.
29. Robert D. Bullard, "Decision Making," in Laura Westra and Peter S. Wenz, eds., *Faces of Environmental Racism: Confronting Issues of Global Justice* (Lanham, MD: Rowman and Littlefield, 1995), 4.
30. Bullard, "Anatomy of Environmental Racism," 21.
31. David L.L. Shields, "What Color Is Hunger?" in David L.L. Shields, ed., *The Color of Hunger: Race and Hunger in National and International Perspective* (Lanham, MD: Rowman and Littlefield, 1996), 4.
32. Centers for Disease Control, "Nutritional Status of Minority Children: United States, 1986," *Morbidity and Mortality Weekly Reports (MMWR)* 36, 23 (June 19, 1987): 366–69.
33. Peter S. Wenz, "Just Garbage," in Laura Westra and Peter S. Wenz, eds., *Faces of Environmental Racism: Confronting Issues of Global Justice* (Lanham, MD: Rowman and Littlefield, 1996), 66; Robert D. Bullard, "Decision Making," in Laura Westra and Peter S. Wenz, eds., *Faces of Environmental Racism,* 8.
34. Laura Pulido, "Multiracial Organizing Among Environmental Justice Activists in Los Angeles," in Michael J. Dear, H. Eric Shockman, and Greg Hise, eds., *Rethinking Los Angeles* (Thousand Oaks, CA, London, New Delhi: Sage, 1996), 175.
35. Charles Trueheart, "The Bias Most Deadly," *Washington Post,* October 30, 1990, sec. 7, cited in Shields, *The Color of Hunger,* 3.
36. George Anders, "Disparities in Medicare Access Found Among Poor, Black or Disabled Patients," *Wall Street Journal,* November 2, 1994; Lina R. Godfrey, "Institutional Discrimination and Satisfaction with Specific Government Services by Heads of Households in Ten Southern States," paper presented at the Rural Sociological Society annual meeting, 1984, cited in Shields, *The Color of Hunger,* 6, 13.
37. Jeffrey Shotland, *Full Fields, Empty Cupboards: The Nutritional Status of Migrant Farm-workers in America* (Washington: Public Voice for Food and Health: 1989) cited in Shields, *The Color of Hunger,* 3.
38. Linda A. Wray, "Health Policy and Ethnic Diversity in Older Americans: Dissonance or Harmony," *Western Journal of Medicine* 157, 3 (September 1992): 357–61.
39. Eva Bertram, Morris Blachman, Kenneth Sharpe, and Peter Andreas, *Drug War Politics: The Price of Denial* (Berkeley and Los Angeles: University of California Press, 1996), 38–42; Alexander C. Lichtenstein and Michael A. Kroll, "The Fortress Economy: The Economic Role of the U.S. Prison System," in Elihu Rosenblatt, ed., *Criminal Injustice: Confronting the Prison Crisis* (Boston: South End, 1996), 21, 25–26.
40. Ibid., 41.
41. Massey and Denton, *American Apartheid,* 61.
42. Gertrude Ezorsky, *Racism and Justice: The Case for Affirmative Action* (Ithaca, NY: Cornell University Press, 1991), 25.
43. Logan and Molotch, *Urban Fortunes,* 116.
44. Jim Campen, "Lending Insights: Hard Proof That Banks Discriminate," *Dollars and Sense,* January–February 1991, 17.
45. Mitchell Zuckoff, "Study Shows Racial Bias in Lending," *Boston Globe,* October 9, 1992.

46. Paul Ong and J. Eugene Grigsby III, "Race and Life-Cycle Effects on Home Ownership in Los Angeles, 1970 to 1980," *Urban Affairs Quarterly* 23, 4 (June 1988): 605.
47. Massey and Denton, *American Apartheid,* 108.
48. Gary Orfield and Carol Ashkinaze, *The Closing Door: Conservative Policy and Black Opportunity* (Chicago: University of Chicago Press, 1991), 58, 78.
49. Logan and Molotch, *Urban Fortunes,* 129.
50. Campen, "Lending Insights," 18.
51. Alicia H. Munnell, Lyn E. Browne, James McEneany, and Geoffrey M.B. Tootel, "Mortgage Lending in Boston: Interpreting HMDA Data" (Boston: Federal Reserve Bank of Boston, 1993); Kimberly Blanton, "Fed Blocks Shawmut's Bid to Gain N.H. Bank," *Boston Globe,* November 16, 1993.
52. Ellis Cose, *Rage of a Privileged Class* (New York: HarperCollins, 1993), 191.
53. Gregory Squires, "'Runaway Plants,' Capital Mobility, and Black Economic Rights," in *Community and Capital in Conflict: Plant Closings and Job Loss,* eds. John C. Raines, Lenora E. Berson, and David McI. Gracie (Philadelphia: Temple University Press, 1983), 70.
54. Ezorsky, *Racism and Justice,* 15.
55. Orfield and Ashkinaze, *The Closing Door,* 225–26.
56. Peter Downs, "Tax Abatements Don't Work," *St. Louis Journalism Review,* February 1997, 16.
57. "State Taxes Gouge the Poor, Study Says," *Long Beach Press-Telegram,* April 23, 1991, sec. A.
58. "Proposition 13," *UC Focus,* June/July 1993, 2.
59. William Chafe, *The Unfinished Journey* (New York: Oxford University Press, 1986), 442; Noel J. Kent, "A Stacked Deck: Racial Minorities and the New American Political Economy," *Explorations in Ethnic Studies* 14, 1 (January 1991): 11.
60. Carey Goldberg, "Hispanic Households Struggle as Poorest of the Poor in the U.S.," *New York Times,* January 30, 1997, sec. A.
61. Kent, "A Stacked Deck," 13.
62. Melvin Oliver and James Johnson, "Economic Restructuring and Black Male Joblessness in United States Metropolitan Areas," *Urban Geography* 12, 6 (November–December 1991); Gerald David Jaynes and Robin M. Williams, Jr., eds., *A Common Destiny: Blacks and American Society* (Washington, D.C.: National Academy Press, 1989); Reynolds Farley and Walter R. Allen, *The Color Line and the Quality of Life in America* (New York: Russell Sage Foundation, 1987); Melvin Oliver and Tom Shapiro, "Wealth of a Nation: A Reassessment of Asset Inequality in America Shows at Least One-Third of Households Are Asset Poor," *Journal of Economics and Sociology* 49, 2 (April 1990); Jonathan Kozol, *Savage Inequalities: Children in America's Schools* (New York: Crown, 1991); Cornell West, *Race Matters* (Boston: Beacon, 1993).
63. Orfield and Ashkinaze, *The Closing Door,* 46, 206.
64. Bart Landry, "The Enduring Dilemma of Race in America," in *America at Century's End,* ed. Alan H. Wolfe (Berkeley and Los Angeles: University of California Press, 1991), 206; John Hope Franklin, *The Color Line: Legacy for the Twenty-First Century* (Columbia: University of Missouri Press, 1993), 36–37.
65. Kathleen Hall Jamieson, *Dirty Politics: Deception, Distraction, and Democracy* (New York: Oxford University Press, 1992), 100.
66. Thomas Byrne Edsall and Mary D. Edsall, *Chain Reaction: The Impact of Race, Rights, and Taxes on American Politics* (New York: Norton, 1991).
67. Nathan Glazer makes this argument in *Affirmative Discrimination* (New York: Basic Books, 1975).
68. I borrow the term "overdetermination" from Louis Althusser, who uses it to show how dominant ideologies become credible to people in part because various institutions and agencies independently replicate them and reinforce their social power.
69. Rogena Schuyler, "Youth: We Didn't Sell Them into Slavery," *Los Angeles Times,* June 21, 1993, sec. B.
70. Jim Newton, "Skinhead Leader Pleads Guilty to Violence, Plot," *Los Angeles Times,* October 20, 1993, sec. A.

71. Antonin Scalia, "The Disease as Cure," *Washington University Law Quarterly,* no. 147 (1979): 153–54, quoted in Cheryl I. Harris, "Whiteness as Property," *Harvard Law Review* 106, 8 (June 1993): 1767.

72. Harris, ibid., 1993.

73. The rise of a black middle class and the setbacks suffered by white workers during deindustrialization may seem to subvert the analysis presented here. Yet the black middle class remains fragile, far less able than other middle-class groups to translate advances in income into advances in wealth and power. Similarly, the success of neoconservatism since the 1970s has rested on securing support from white workers for economic policies that do them objective harm by mobilizing counter-subversive electoral coalitions against busing and affirmative action, while carrying out attacks on public institutions and resources by representing "public" space as black space. See Oliver and Shapiro, "Wealth of a Nation." See also Logan and Molotch, *Urban Fortunes.*

CHAPTER 10

The Perils of Color Blindness

Dottie Blais

One Friday morning, right after teaching my third-period English class, I came face-to-face with my own racial and cultural prejudices.

I had just delivered a well-intentioned diatribe about the consequences of not doing homework. I couldn't understand why so many tenth graders were simply not reading their short-story assignments, or if they read them, were showing so little enthusiasm in class discussions.

One student, Julian, had remained in his seat after I dismissed the class. I sensed he had something to say.

Finally, he stood up and approached my desk. Julian was a tall, African American sixteen-year-old with intelligent eyes, one of my favorite students.

"You ought to quit trying to make us white," he said matter-of-factly. "All these stories you're making us read are by white people, about white people." His eyes pointed to the open textbook on my desk.

"Julian, I didn't select these stories on the basis of race," I said emphatically, stunned by the implications of racism. It was the unpardonable sin in a school where 70 percent of the students were ethnic minorities.

"Maybe you should have," he said, almost in a whisper, and left the classroom to silence.

I struggled to comprehend. His suggestion was inconceivable, especially since I had always prided myself on conducting "color-blind" classes.

I picked up the textbook and turned to the table of contents. Scanning titles and authors, I suddenly realized the awful truth. I hadn't deliberately eliminated writers of other ethnicities, but I hadn't deliberately included them either. Clearly, the assignments reflected my own unconscious cultural biases, and one student had the courage to say so.

Like many other well-intentioned educators, I had fully embraced the concept of color blindness. In theory, the approach sounds good. In a world where racial conflict has been such a problem, why wouldn't color blindness—with its attempt to remove race from the classroom altogether—be the perfect way to ensure that racism never rears its ugly head?

What I didn't realize until the incident with Julian is that color blindness has an ugliness of its own. The paradoxical truth, according to a 2004 study by Northwestern University psychologist Jennifer Richeson and her colleague Richard Nussbaum, is that the ideology of color blindness may cause more rather than less racial bias, a result that echoes other research findings.

How is that possible? To understand how a perspective intended to avoid racism in the classroom can actually encourage racism, educators must examine their own motives for employing the strategy, and several recent studies of color blindness can help them do so.

"The Perils of Color Blindness" by Dottie Blais. From *Greater Good*, the magazine of the University of California at Berkeley's Greater Good Science Center. Reprinted by permission.

Teachers may believe, as I once did, that if they could somehow not see the race of their students, then they couldn't possibly be racist. However, a wave of new research has found that one of the first and most automatic ways people respond to others is to categorize them by race, even if they wish it were otherwise. In other words, achieving true color blindness is virtually impossible.

To deny what they inevitably see, many people employ what researchers call "strategic" color blindness, a strategy that requires maintaining an Orwellian perspective on race—that is, seeing and not seeing at the same time—to avoid the appearance of racism.

This is a recipe for disaster. In fact, a 2006 *Psychological Science* paper by Harvard University psychologist Michael Norton and colleagues reveals just how much this race-denying strategy can impair interracial communication. In one of their studies, white college-age students were randomly paired with a black or white partner (actually a confederate in the study, working with the researchers). Together they played a "political correctness" game: the white student had to examine thirty-two photographs that differed in three ways—by the gender of the subject, the color of the background, or the race of the subject. The black or white partner was given six of these thirty-two photos, and the object of the game was for the white "questioner" to identify the individual photos the "answerer" was looking at by asking as few yes/no questions about the photos as possible.

When whites were paired with whites, they were quick to ask about the race of the person depicted in each photo. But when they were paired with a black partner, they were significantly less likely to invoke race, even if their failure to do so meant scoring poorly in the game.

What's more, when whites tried to avoid mentioning race to black partners, their nonverbal behavior would change for the worse—they'd make less eye contact, for instance—and their communication in general would seem less friendly. Whites simply would not risk being perceived as racist, even though ignoring race in the game negatively affected their performance and their interactions with their partner.

A 2008 study published in the *Journal of Personality and Social Psychology* took Norton's research a step further, examining the effects that whites' attempts at color blindness had on black participants. Ironically, the negative nonverbal behaviors exhibited by "color-blind" whites were interpreted by blacks as signs of prejudice, making them suspicious of their partners. It is hardly surprising that racial tensions increased among participants.

What do these research findings mean for educators who truly want to avoid racism in the classroom? It seems clear that adopting a color-blind perspective, though often well intentioned and arguably a step in the right direction, does not actually combat prejudice among students and faculty; instead, it exacerbates racial divisions. We should abandon this practice. In its place, research suggests that a multicultural perspective, encouraging recognition and celebration of differences, is much more likely to reduce racial tensions and promote interracial communication. (See Jennifer Holladay's essay in this collection for more on the multicultural perspective.)

In retrospect, I can understand why Julian and other minority students in my English classroom were seething with resentment. By refusing to acknowledge that they were different from me, I elicited suspicion and discomfort. What's more, I insulted their racial and cultural identity. My color blindness signaled to them that they were invisible, somehow unworthy of my attention and my curriculum; my efforts were perceived as an attempt to "whiten" them.

Julian was right. If I had chosen to acknowledge race in my classroom, I could have intentionally developed a curriculum that was more inclusive. I could have provided an opportunity for students of all races to explore their own cultures through literature that extended and enriched the traditional canon. I could have used diversity as a learning opportunity for everyone in the classroom, including myself.

Julian taught me that if we choose not to acknowledge race in the classroom, students and teachers will rarely confront their own prejudices. Tolerance results from seeing commonalities. But unless we first see ourselves as different, we will never see ourselves as the same.

Library of Congress

Questions for Discussion

Blair notes how her literary selections for her classes unconsciously reflected the perspectives of white people to the exclusion of people of color. Think about how you have been taught about American history, both in school and through popular media as you answer these questions.

1. Whose perspective has dominated? Who are the actors at the center of the story?

2. Think about films that deal with interactions among different racial groups. Who starred in them? From whose perspective was the story told? How would those films have been different if told from another perspective?

3. Think about famous historical (or partly historical) events, such as Columbus's voyages, the first Thanksgiving, the Lewis and Clark expedition, the Civil War, the Great Depression, or the 1950s. Who is at the center of these stories as you have heard them?

4. Has America's history been told in a colorblind manner? Can it be?

CHAPTER 11

How White People Can Serve as Allies to People of Color in the Struggle to End Racism

Paul Kivel

What Does an Ally Do?

Being allies to people of color in the struggle to end racism is one of the most important things that white people can do. There is no one correct way to be an ally. Each of us is different. We have different relationships to social organizations, political processes, and economic structures. We are more or less powerful because of such factors as our gender, class, work situation, family, and community participation. Being an ally to people of color is an ongoing strategic process in which we look at our personal and social resources, evaluate the environment we have helped to create and decide what needs to be done.

Times change and circumstances vary. What is a priority today may not be tomorrow. What is effective or strategic right now may not be next year. We need to be thinking with others and noticing what is going on around us so we will know how to put our attention, energy, time, and money toward strategic priorities in the struggle to end racism and other injustices.

This includes listening to people of color so that we can support the actions they take, the risks they bear in defending their lives and challenging white hegemony. It includes watching the struggle of white people to maintain dominance and the struggle of people of color to gain equal opportunity, justice, safety, and respect.

We don't need to believe or accept as true everything people of color say. There is no one voice in any community, much less in the complex and diverse communities of color spanning our country. We do need to listen carefully to the voices of people of color so that we understand and give credence to their experience. We can then evaluate the content of what they are saying by what we know about how racism works and by our own critical thinking and progressive political analysis.

It is important to emphasize this point because often we become paralyzed when people of color talk about racism. We are afraid to challenge what they say. We will be ineffective as allies if we give up our ability to analyze and think critically, if we simply accept everything that a person of color states as truth.

Listening to people of color and giving critical credence to their experience is not easy for us because of the training we have received. Nevertheless, it is an important first step. When we hear statements that make us want to react defensively, we can instead keep some specific things in mind as we try to understand what is happening and determine how best to be allies.

We have seen how racism is a pervasive part of our culture. Therefore we should always assume that racism is at least part of the picture. In light of this assumption, we should look for the patterns involved rather than treating most events as isolated occurrences.

Since we know that racism is involved, we know our whiteness is also a factor. We should look for ways we are acting from assumptions of white power or privilege. This will help us acknowledge any fear or confusion we may feel. It will allow us to see our tendencies to defend ourselves or our tendencies to assume we should be in control. Then we will be able to talk with other white people so these tendencies don't get in the way of our being effective allies.

We have many opportunities to practice these critical listening and thinking skills because we are all involved in a complex web of interpersonal and institutional relationships. Every day we are presented with opportunities to analyze what is going on around us and to practice taking direct action as allies to people of color.

People of color will always be on the front lines fighting racism because their lives are at stake. How do we act and support them effectively, both when they are in the room with us, and when they are not?

It can be difficult for those of us who are white to know how to be strong allies for people of color when discrimination occurs. In the following interaction, imagine that Roberto is a young Latino student just coming out of a job interview with a white recruiter from a computer company. Let's see how one white person might respond.

Roberto is angry, not sure what to do next. He walks down the hall and meets a white teacher who wants to help.[1]

R = Roberto, **T** = teacher

T: Hey, Roberto, how's it going?

R: That son of a bitch! He wasn't going to give me no job. That was really messed up.

T: Hold on there, don't be so angry. It was probably a mistake or something.

R: There was no mistake. The racist bastard. He wants to keep me from getting a good job, rather have us all on welfare or doing maintenance work.

T: Calm down now or you'll get yourself in more trouble. Don't go digging a hole for yourself. Maybe I could help you if you weren't so angry.

R: That's easy for you to say. This man was discriminating against me. White folks are all the same. They talk about equal opportunity, but it's the same old shit.

T: Wait a minute, I didn't have anything to do with this. Don't blame me, I'm not responsible. If you wouldn't be so angry maybe I could help you. You probably took what he said the wrong way. Maybe you were too sensitive.

R: I could tell. He was racist. That's all. (He storms off.)

What did you notice about this scene? On the one hand the teacher is concerned and is trying to help. On the other hand his intervention is not very effective. He immediately downplays the incident, discounting Roberto's feelings and underestimating the possibility of racism. He seems to be saying that racism is unlikely—it was probably just a misunderstanding, or Roberto was being too sensitive.

The teacher is clearly uncomfortable with Roberto's anger. He begins to defend himself, the job recruiter, and white people. He ends up feeling attacked for being white. Rather than talking about what happened, he focuses on Roberto's anger and his generalizations about white people. By the end of the interaction he is threatening to get Roberto in trouble himself if he doesn't calm down. As he walks away he may be thinking it's no wonder Roberto didn't get hired for the job.

You probably recognize some of the tactics described. The teacher denies or minimizes the likelihood of racism, blames Roberto, and eventually counterattacks, claiming to be a victim of Roberto's anger and racial generalizations.

This interaction illustrates some of our common feelings that get in the way of intervening effectively where discrimination is occurring. First is the feeling that we are being personally attacked. It is difficult to hear the phrase "all white people," or "you white people." We want to defend ourselves and other whites. We don't want to believe that white people could intentionally hurt others. Or we may want to say, "Not me, I'm different."

There are some things we should remember when we feel attacked. First, this is a question of injustice. We need to focus on what happened and what we can do about it, not on our feelings of being attacked.

Second, someone who has been the victim of injustice is legitimately angry and they may or may not express that anger in ways we like. Criticizing the way people express their anger deflects attention and action away from the injustice that was committed. After the injustice has been dealt with, if you still think it's worthwhile and not an attempt to control the situation yourself, you can go back and discuss ways of expressing anger.

Often, because we are frequently complacent about injustice that doesn't affect us directly, it takes a lot of anger and aggressive action to bring attention to a problem. If we were more proactive in identifying and intervening in situations of injustice, people would not have to be so "loud" to get our attention in the first place.

Finally, part of the harm that racism does is that it forces people of color to be wary and mistrustful of all white people, just as sexism forces women to mistrust all men. People of color face racism every day, often from unexpected quarters. They never know when a white friend, coworker, teacher, police officer, doctor, or passer-by may discriminate, act hostile, or say something offensive. They have to be wary of *all* white people, even though they know that not all white people will mistreat them. They have likely been hurt in the past by white people they thought they could trust, and therefore they may make statements about all white people. We must remember that although we want to be trustworthy, trust is not the issue. We are not fighting racism so that people of color will trust us. Trust builds over time through our visible efforts to be allies and fight racism. Rather than trying to be safe and trustworthy, we need to be more active, less defensive, and put issues of trust aside.

When people are discriminated against they may feel unseen, stereotyped, attacked or as if a door has been slammed in their face. They may feel confused, frustrated, helpless, or angry. They are probably reminded of other similar experiences. They may want to hurt someone in return, or hide their pain, or simply forget about the whole experience. Whatever the response, the experience is deeply wounding and painful. It is an act of emotional violence.

It's also an act of economic violence to be denied access to a job, housing, educational program, pay raise, or promotion that one deserves. It is a practice which keeps economic resources in the hands of one group and denies them to another.

When a person is discriminated against it is a serious event and we need to treat it seriously. It is also a common event. For instance, the government estimates that there are over two million acts of race-based housing discrimination every year—twenty million every decade (Ezorsky p. 13). We know that during their lifetimes people of color have to face many such discriminatory experiences in school, work, housing, and community settings.

People of color do not protest discrimination lightly. They know that when they do white people routinely deny or minimize it, blame them for causing trouble and then counterattack. This is the "happy family" syndrome described earlier.

People of color are experts in discrimination resulting from racism. Most experience it regularly and see its effects on their communities. Not every complaint of discrimination is valid, but most have some truth in them. It would be a tremendous step forward if we assumed that there was some truth in every complaint of racial discrimination even when other factors may also be involved. At least then we would take it seriously enough to fully investigate.

How could the teacher in the above scenario be a better ally to Roberto? We can go back to the guidelines suggested earlier for help. First, he needs to listen much more carefully to what Roberto is saying. He should assume that Roberto is intelligent, and if he says there was racism involved then there probably was. The teacher should be aware of his own power and position, his tendency to be defensive and his desire to defend other white people or presume their innocence. It would also be worthwhile to look for similar occurrences because racism is usually not an isolated instance, but a pattern within an organization or institution.

Let's see how these suggestions might operate in a replay of this scene.

T: Hey, Roberto, what's happening?

R: That son of a bitch! He wasn't going to give me no job. He was messin' with me.

T: You're really upset, tell me what happened.

R: He was discriminating against me. Wasn't going to hire me cause I'm Latino. White folks are all alike. Always playing games.

T: This is serious. Why don't you come into my office and tell me exactly what happened.

R: Okay. This company is advertising for computer programmers and I'm qualified for the job. But this man tells me there aren't any computer jobs, and then he tries to steer me toward a janitor job. He was a racist bastard.

T: That's tough. I know you would be good in that job. This sounds like a case of job discrimination. Let's write down exactly what happened, and then you can decide what you want to do about it.

R: I want to get that job.

T: If you want to challenge it, I'll help you. Maybe there's something we can do.

This time the teacher was being a strong, supportive ally to Roberto.

I Would Be a Perfect Ally If . . .

We learn many excuses and justifications for racism in this society. We also learn many tactics for avoiding responsibility for it. We have developed a coded language to help us avoid even talking about it directly. Our training makes it easy to find reasons for not being allies to people of color. In order to maintain our commitment to being allies, we must reject the constant temptation to find excuses for being inactive.

What reasons have you used for not taking a stronger stand against racism, or for backing away from supporting a person of color?

Following are some of the reasons I've recently heard white people use. I call them "if only" statements because that's the phrase they usually begin with. Our real meaning is just the reverse. We are often setting conditions on our commitment to racial justice. We are saying that "only if" people of color do this or that will we do our part. These conditions let us blame people of color for our not being reliable allies.

I would be a committed and effective ally:

- If only people of color weren't so angry, sensitive, impatient, or demanding;
- If only people of color realized that I am different from other white people, I didn't own slaves, I treat everyone the same, I don't see color, I'm not a member of the KKK and I've even been to an unlearning racism workshop;
- If only people of color would give white people a chance, hear our side of things and realize that we have it hard too;
- If only people of color didn't use phrases like "all white people";
- If only people of color didn't expect the government to do everything for them and wouldn't ask for special treatment.

Being a white ally to people of color means to be there all the time, for the long term, committed and active. Because this is hard, challenging work, we often look for ways to justify not doing it. Rather than finding ways to avoid being allies, we need to look at what gets in our way. Where does it get hard? Where do we get stuck? Many of the reasons listed above are ways to justify withdrawal from the struggle against racism.

Another way we justify our withdrawal is to find a person of color who represents, in our minds, the reason why people of color don't really deserve our support. Often these examples have to do with people of color not spending money or time the way we think they should. "I know a person who spends all her money on. . . ."

We often set standards for their conduct that we haven't previously applied to white people in the same position. "Look what happened when so-and-so got into office." In most instances we are criticizing a person of color for not being perfect (by our standards), and then using that person as an example of an entire group of people.

People of color are not perfect. Within each community of color people are as diverse as white people, with all the human strengths and failings. The question is one of justice. No one should have to earn justice. We don't talk about taking away rights or opportunities from white people because we don't like them, or because they don't make the decisions we think they should. Even when white people break the law, are obviously incompetent for the position they hold, are mean, cruel or inept, it is often difficult to hold them accountable for their actions. Our laws call for equal treatment of everyone. We should apply the same standards and treatments to people of color as we do to white people.

Not only are people of color not perfect, neither are they representatives of their race. Yet how many times have we said,

- "But I know a person of color who . . . "
- "A person of color told me that . . . "
- "So and so is a credit to her race . . . "
- (Turning to an individual) "What do people of color think about that . . . ?"
- "Let's ask so and so, he's a person of color."

We would never say that a white person was representative of that race, even if that person were Babe Ruth, Mother Teresa, Hitler, John Lennon, or Margaret Thatcher, much less the only white person in the room. When was the last time you spoke as a representative for white people?

Imagine yourself in a room of fifty people where you are the only white person. At one point in the middle of a discussion about a major issue, the facilitator turns to you and says, "Could you please tell us what white people think about this issue?" How would you feel? What would you say? Would it make any difference if the facilitator said, "I know you can't speak for other white people, but could you tell us what the white perspective is on this issue?" What support would you want from other people around you in the room?

In that situation would you want a person of color to be your ally by interrupting the racial dynamic and pointing out that there isn't just one white perspective, and you couldn't represent white people? Would you want them to challenge the other people present and stand up for you? Being a white ally to people of color calls for the same kind of intervention—stepping in to support people of color when we see any kind of racism being played out.

Basic Tactics

Every situation is different and calls for critical thinking about how to make a difference. Taking the statements above into account, I have compiled some general guidelines.

1. **Assume racism is everywhere, everyday.** Just as economics influences everything we do, just as our gender and gender politics influence everything we do, assume that racism is affecting whatever is going on. We assume this because it's true, and because one of the privileges of being white is not having to see or deal with racism all the time. We have to learn to see the effect that racism has. Notice who speaks, what is said, how things are done and described. Notice who isn't present. Notice code words for race, and the implications of the policies, patterns and comments that are being expressed. You already notice the skin color of everyone you meet and interact with—now notice what difference it makes.

2. **Notice who is the center of attention and who is the center of power.** Racism works by directing violence and blame toward people of color and consolidating power and privilege for white people.

3. **Notice how racism is denied, minimized, and justified.**

4. **Understand and learn from the history of whiteness and racism.** Notice how racism has changed over time and how it has subverted or resisted challenges. Study the tactics that have worked effectively against it.

5. **Understand the connections between racism, economic issues, sexism, and other forms of injustice.**

6. **Take a stand against injustice.** Take risks. It is scary, difficult, risky and may bring up many feelings, but ultimately it is the only healthy and moral human thing to do. Intervene in situations where racism is being passed on.

7. **Be strategic.** Decide what is important to challenge and what's not. Think about strategy in particular situations. Attack the source of power.

8. **Don't confuse a battle with the war.** Behind particular incidents and interactions are larger patterns. Racism is flexible and adaptable. There will be gains and losses in the struggle for justice and equality.

9. **Don't call names or be personally abusive.** Since power is often defined as power over others—the ability to abuse or control people—it is easy to become abusive ourselves. However, we usually end up abusing people who have less power than we do because it is less dangerous. Attacking people doesn't address the systemic nature of racism and inequality.

10. **Support the leadership of people of color.** Do this consistently, but not uncritically.

11. **Don't do it alone.** You will not end racism by yourself. We can do it if we work together. Build support, establish networks, work with already established groups.

12. **Talk with your children and other young people about racism.**

Reference

Ezorsky, Gertrude. *Racism and Justice: The Case for Affirmative Action.* Ithaca, NY: Cornell University Press, 1991.

Note

1. Adapted from *Men's Work: How to Stop the Violence That Tears Our Lives Apart* (Hazelden/Ballantine, 1992).

CPSIA information can be obtained
at www.ICGtesting.com
Printed in the USA
LVHW060355260419
615401LV00002B/2/P

9 781465 292384